Landscapes of the
COSTA BLANCA

a countryside guide
Sixth edition

John and Christine Oldfield
revised by Sunflower Books

SUNFLOWER BOOKS

Sixth edition © 2025
Sunflower Books™
PO Box 36160
London SW7 3WS, UK
www.sunflowerbooks.co.uk

ISBN 978-1-85691-565-6

Well at Caprala (Walk 24)

Important note to the reader

We have tried to ensure that the descriptions and maps in this book are error-free at press date. The book will be updated, where necessary, whenever future editions permit. It is very helpful for us to receive your comments (sent to info@sunflowerbooks.co.uk, please) for the updating of future editions.

We also rely on those who use this book — especially walkers — to take along a good supply of common sense when they explore. Conditions change fairly rapidly in these mountains, and *storm damage or bulldozing may make a route unsafe at any time*. If the route is not as we outline it here, and your way ahead is not secure, return to the point of departure. *Never attempt to complete a tour or walk under hazardous conditions!* Please read carefully the notes on pages 39 to 44, as well as the introductory comments at the beginning of each tour and walk (regarding road conditions, equipment, grade, distances and time, etc). Explore *safely*, while at the same time respecting the beauty of the countryside.

Cover photograph: Tarbena (Car tour 3)
Title page: The Cavall Verd ('Green Horse') rises beyond almond blossom (Car tours 1 and 3)

Photographs by the authors, except for pages 16-7, 21, 33, 42, 56, 90-1, 123, 134 and the cover: Shutterstock
Maps by Sunflower Books (walking maps adapted from Spanish military maps, with kind permission of the Servicio Geográfico del Ejército)
A CIP catalogue record for this book is available from the British Library.
Printed and bound in England by Short Run Press, Exeter

Contents

Preface — 5
Acknowledgements — 5
Language, place names and glossary — 5
Snow wells — 6

Getting about — 8
Plans of Alicante, Benidorm and Dénia — 8

Picnicking — 10
A country code for walkers, motorists and picnickers — 11
Picnic suggestions — 12

Touring — 16
1 COSTA BLANCA NEW AND OLD — 18
2 NORTHERN VALLEYS — THE CHERRY ROUTE — 24
3 CENTRAL VALLEYS — THE ALMOND ROUTE — 27
4 SOUTHERN VALLEYS AND WESTERN HIGHLANDS — 30
5 EL CID COUNTRY — 36

Walking (● see explanation of grading symbols on page 40) — 39
Grading, waymarking, maps, GPS — 40
Where to stay — 41
Weather — 41
What to take — 42
Nuisances — 43
Organisation of the walks — 44

WALKS ON THE COASTAL STRIP: DENIA TO BENIDORM
● 1 Montgó — 45
● 2 Short walks around Xàbia and Calp — 47
● 3 Vuelta de Oltá (Oltá circuit) — 51
● 4 The four faces of Puig Campana — 54
● 5 Serra Gelada — from Benidorm to Albir — 56

WALKS IN THE SERPIS AND GALLINERA VALLEYS
● 6 Serpis Gorge — 59
● 7 Serra de La Safor — 62
● 8 Barranc de la Encantada and Ermita de Santo Cristo — 65
● 9 L'Atzubia • Castell de Gallinera • Miserat • L'Atzubia — 68

WALKS IN THE LAGUAR AND JALON VALLEYS
● 10 Serra de la Carrasca and the Mozarabic trails — 73
● 11 Vuelta del Somo (Somo circuit) — 77
● 12 Fonts de l'Algar • Serra de Bérnia • Barranc de Binarreal • Fonts de l'Algar — 80

**WALKS IN THE GUADALEST, ALGAR AND
SELLA VALLEYS**

13 Valleys of the Serra de Aitana   85
14 Penya Sella   88
15 Presa de Guadalest   90
16 The *font* circuit
                                                                         93

WALKS IN THE ALCOI AREA
17 Camí de l'Escaleta and the old road: circuit from Bocairent   96
18 Alcoi • Barranc del Sinc • Coll Sabata • Montcabrer •
    Racó Llobet • Muro de Alcoi   99
19 The *cavas*: circuit from Agres   105
20 Font Mariola • Ermita de San Tomás • El Portín •
    Alt de la Cova • Cova de Bolumini • Font Mariola   109
21 Parc Natural de Font Roja   112
22 Penàguila Castle
                                                                        117

**WALKS IN THE SERRAS OF CARRASQUETA
AND MAIGMO**
23 La Carrasqueta: Port de la Carrasqueta • Pou del Surdo •
    Mas de la Cova • Port de la Carrasqueta   119
24 Elda • L'Arenal • Caprala • Rambla dels Molins • Petrer • Elda   122
25 Castalla • Fermosas Plateau • Pantanet Gorge • Catí •
    Despeñador • Castalla   126
26 Serra del Frare   131

Bus and train timetables   133
Index (of geographical names)   135
Touring map   *inside back cover*

Cherry orchards near L'Orxa, with Benicadell rising in the distance (Car tour 2)

Preface

The pleasure of researching and writing the First edition of this book a couple of decades ago has been amply rewarded over the years by the correspondence we have received from users. We no longer live in Spain, but always enjoy returning to the mountains and valleys of the Costa Blanca where we regularly meet people using the guide and can learn from their experiences and recommendations. In the meantime, please *do* keep sending your comments to Sunflower Books for their Update Service.

This Sixth edition has been updated by the team at Sunflower; several of the changes have come from your suggestions — and from the great number of new trails developed by local councils. There is now a huge number of possibilities which did not exist when we first wrote the book — thanks both to EU funding and to the fact that so many people have realised the incredible beauty of this region and its attraction for walkers.

When we first wrote this book, it was the *only* guide to hiking in the Costa Blanca. Since then several guides have come on the market. All have a slightly different approach and — aside from the 'must-do' hikes — each has a surprisingly different selection of walks. So rather than try to include even more walks in this Sixth edition (since the possibilities are seemingly *endless*), Sunflower's editors have concentrated on bringing the existing routes up to date, updating the maps and improving them with waypoints, and offering free GPS tracks for all the routes.

Acknowledgements

The original book was written with the invaluable assistance of the Centro Excursionista de Valencia, Rafael Cebrián, Eric Wright and Ross Gow. Subsequent editions owe much to the many users who have taken the time to contact us or the team at Sunflower Books.

Language, place names and glossary

Many people on the tourist beat speak English, but that is not the case when you leave the coast. A simple Spanish phrase book or smartphone translator can be invaluable — although many older people speak Valenciano and are uncomfortable with Spanish.

In the Costa Blanca region you will quickly become aware that place names may have two different spellings — **Castellano** (Spanish as we know it) and **Valenciano**. Mostly the two are very similar, with just an omitted letter or added accent, but in a few cases they can be quite different, for example Jávea becomes Xábia, Jijona Xixona. The revival of Valenciano means that Castilian names are gradually being phased

Serra de Aitana

out, but some towns and features are still known by their Castilian names. In this book we use the version you are most likely to encounter, but give both versions where confusion might occur.

Some of the older settlements have rather long names, but it is

SNOW WELLS *(casas de nieve, neveras, pous, cavas, cavetas)*
Several of our walks feature well-preserved *pous* or *cavas*, and you will be amazed by their size and the solidity of their construction. Before the days of the refrigerator, snow was commercially 'harvested', compacted in a well and left till summer, when it was cut into blocks of ice. During the coolest time of the day, usually in the hours of darkness, the ice was transported down the mountains by mule, donkey or cart, to the distant towns. These wells are described by different names, depending on their location — for example those on the Carrasqueta Ridge are called *pous*, while those around Agres are called *cavas*. High in the mountains, walls were built in strategic locations to catch the drifting snow and, whenever there had been a significant fall, men would be hired to shovel it into a *pou* and press it down. These *pous* were sometimes just natural dips in the ground but, more often, were

customary to abbreviate them. We have used full names once only. For instance, after mentioning Planes de la Baronía, we refer to it thereafter simply as Planes. There are many place names beginning with 'Beni', for example Bernialí, Benirrama, Benitaia. These are relics of the Moorish occupation, the prefix being comparable to the Scottish 'Mac'.

In the course of the text, where it 'felt right', we have used some local words instead of the English equivalent. In the glossary below we give their meaning.

ambiente atmosphere
arroyo stream
autovía dual carriageway
ayuntamiento, ajuntament town hall
barra French stick, baguette
barranco, barranc gorge, ravine, gully
bocadillo sandwich (often half a *barra*)
bodega wine cellar/shop
cabo, cap cape
calle, carrer street
camino, camí small street, path
camino rural country road
canaleta small water channel
casa/casita house/little house
castillo, castell castle
cava/caveta snow well (see below)
cerro hill
coll, collado hill or saddle
corral farm
correos post office
coto privado de caza private hunting
  reserve
cueva, cova cave
embalse, presa reservoir
ermita hermitage or chapel
finca farmhouse and farm
fuente, font spring
gasoleo diesel

gasolina petrol
hostal cheap hotel
hoya, foia valley, basin
huerta market garden
lavadero wash-house
levante east
masía, mas farm
mirador viewpoint
molino, molí windmill
nao ship
nevera snow well (see below)
peña, penya rock
piscina swimming pool
playa, platja beach
plaza square
puerto, port mountain pass (or seaport)
pou snow well (see below)
puig mountain
río, riu river
salinas saltpans
santuario, santuari sanctuary or
  hermitage
tapas snacks or appetizers
torrente dry river bed
turrón almond sweetmeat
valle, vall valley
vuelta circuit

specially constructed for the purpose. Pits were dug, usually cylindrical in form, and when full of snow were covered with brushwood and branches to ward off the worst of the summer heat. More sophisticated wells were covered by a stone hut with a conical roof and two or three access doors. Stone steps or iron rungs would be set into the walls of the pit to enable the pressers and block-cutters to get down to the snow level, and special tools were used to cut the blocks.

Caveta del Buitre (Walk 19)

Getting about

There is a reasonable bus service between the main centres on the coast and some of the larger inland towns, but in the mountain regions bus times are not designed to suit walkers. However, it is possible to reach some of our walks by **bus**, and we have included the relevant timetables on pages 133-134. Timetables can vary, depending on the season, so visit local bus stations for up-to-date information or download timetables from the web in advance (see page 133).

A few walks are also accessible by **train** or by the **narrow-gauge railway** called **TRAM** which runs up and down the coast between Alicante (where it *is* a tram) to Benidorm (where you change to a train) and on to Dénia, stopping at every imaginable place en route and affording leisurely views of coastline and countryside. For some of the walks you could make use of a **taxi**, or arrange to stay overnight close to the area where they start.

The most practical option is to **hire a car**. This way you are free to stop at will to admire a view, fill up water bottles at road-side *fonts*, or explore some of the fascinating villages through which you will pass. Cars are most economically hired before you travel, when you book your flight. Alternatively, in the coastal towns, there are many companies vying for your business with special offers and discounts. But make sure you know exactly what you are paying for before hiring; the price quoted may not include collision damage waiver or unlimited mileage!

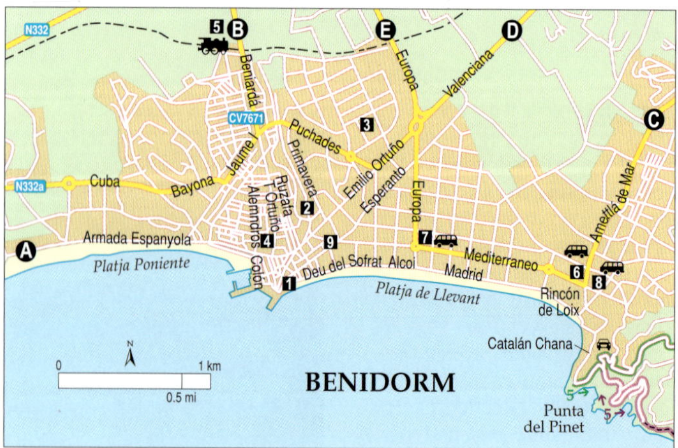

BENIDORM KEY	ALICANTE KEY	DENIA KEY
1 Tourist office	1 Tourist office	1 Railway station and tourist information
2 Town hall	2 Town hall	2 Dénia castle
3 Police	3 Market	3 Creu Roja (Red Cross)
4 Market	4 Bullring	4 MAPFRE roundabout
5 Railway station	5 RENFE train station	5 Al Khalif mosque
6 Albir buses	6 FGV railway station	6 Alqueries station
7 ALSA buses	7 Murcia railway station	
8 Guadalest buses	8 Bus station	
9 Plaza de la Hispanidad	9 Post office	
	10 Cathedral	
	11 Museum	

Picnicking

We have found some spectacular picnic spots during our walks through the mountains in this area of Spain. They should appeal to those who prefer *very* short walks. If you are car touring, they are an 'off-the-beaten-track' alternative to the area's designated picnic sites, mostly by the roadside, with benches and bins (indicated in the touring notes with the symbol ⍐). These tend to get quite busy on Sundays and *fiestas*. How much better it is to get away from the trappings of civilisation and enjoy a picnic in the wilderness, watching a stream flow by, admiring a mountain view or listening to the birds!

All the information you need to find these more secluded picnic spots is given below, where *picnic numbers correspond to walk numbers,* so you can quickly find their general location by looking at the touring map (where walk areas are highlighted). We give you walking times and transport details. The precise location of the picnic spot is indicated by the symbol *P* on the appropriate *walking map,* which also shows the nearest 🚗 parking place and 🚐 stop (if accessible by bus).

Please remember to **wear sensible shoes** and **take a sunhat**. It's a good idea to take a groundsheet as well, in case it's damp or prickly. Take food *with you* too; don't rely on buying it en route. There aren't always shops in the inland villages, and their range may be limited. A fresh *barra* (baguette), a hunk of cheese, a couple of tomatoes and some fresh fruit make a satisfying feast. We always carry a small sharp knife, salt and paper towels, to avoid making up sandwiches in advance.

At some of the picnic sites there are *fonts*, so you can enjoy a refreshing cool drink with your food and refill your water bottles. But after long droughts and in the height of summer some *fonts* might run dry; do not *rely* on them as your only source of liquid on a trip. And, of course, leave no rubbish behind, even if others have done so before you.

All picnickers should heed the country code on the facing page.

Right: Montgó from the highest point on Cap Prim (Walk 2c — and just a short stroll from the setting for Picnic 2c)

A country code for walkers, motorists and picnickers

The Spanish countryside is essentially unspoiled. It is only around the more accessible, and therefore popular, picnic or camping areas that you will come across litter. Please do not be tempted to add to it. Fire is a major hazard in countryside that is always parched during the summer months (and, in these days of climate change, sometimes all year round after a drought). Respect this country code and ensure that this beautiful area remains unspoiled.

- **Take all your litter away with you.**
- **Do not light fires or throw away cigarette ends.**
- **Protect all wild and cultivated plants.** Don't pick wild flowers. Never cross cultivated land, and do not be tempted to pick cherries, citrus fruits, almonds or olives — these are clearly someone's private property.
- **Do not disturb or frighten animals or birds.**
- **Protect water sources.** *Fonts* (springs) in the mountains are especially important. When attending to 'calls of nature' keep well away from springs and streams, and make sure that you bury all paper.
- **Walkers — do not take risks!** Never walk alone and always tell someone where you are going and when you expect to return. It might be helpful also to leave this information on a note in your hotel room. Remember that any route could become dangerous after storms or bull-dozing. If you are lost or injured you may have to wait a long time for help. *Deep gorges* should always be treated with care and caution. Walkers have disappeared or died in the mountains of the Costa Blanca. Usually the cause of these accidents is carelessness and lack of common sense.

2b XABIA'S *MOLINS* (map on page 48, photo on page 50)

🚗 car to the Santuario de Nuestra Señora de los Angeles on the Cap de Sant Antoni road (Car tour 1); 21min on foot from the Santuario, or 12min if you drive up to the crest (limited parking). Walk up Camí del Monastir, then follow Walk 2b from the 25min-point (page 48). No shade, but rocky plinths to sit on and fantastic views across Xàbia Bay.

2c CREU DEL PORTITXOL (*map on page 49, photo on page 11*)

🚗 car from Xàbia (Car tour 1); 4min or 21min on foot. Follow Walk 2c (page 49) for 4min, to picnic on the grassy terraces or at the cliff edge. Shade of pines if you want it, magnificent views, lovely ambience. Or follow Walk 2c for about 10min, then take the eroded path on the left which leads to steps down to Cala Sardinera (21min), a secluded pebbly beach, with clear water. No shade.

2d CALP CALAS (*map on page 49*)

🚗 by car or 🚌 bus to Cala Calalga (30km point on Car tour 1); up to 54min on foot. Follow Walk 2d (page 50). Every cove is a possible picnic spot, but we particularly recommend the one at the end of the walk. It's secluded, there are flat rocks to sit on, and the location and views are fantastic. No shade.

3 ERMITA VELLA (*map on page 52*)

🚗 by car to Calp station (Car tour 1), then drive to the alternative starting point for Walk 3 (see page 51). Follow the walk to the 33min-point; 20min on foot. There are well laid out picnic benches, toilets, an 'old' (2003 vintage!) *ermita* and great views.

5 PUNTA DE LA ESCALETA, SERRA GELADA (*map on page 57*)

🚗 by car, taxi or on foot to Benidorm's Playa Levante (Car tour 1). You can either drive to within 200m of the picnic spot, or follow coastal paths for 40min. Follow Short walk 5-2 (page 56). This rocky promontory offers no shade, but there are magnificent views round the coast to Benidorm. You could also follow a path up to the 17th-century *torre,* to look out to the cliffs of the Serra Gelada.

6a, b SERPIS RIVER (*map pages 60-1*)

🚗 to L'Orxa station (Car tour 2);

Picnic 10b: The lavadero *at Fleix*

either 12min or 46min on foot. (a) Follow Walk 6 (page 59) for 9min, then take the track to the right. In a few minutes you will come to abandoned grassy terraces on the left overlooking the river, with shade from olive trees. (b) Follow the walk to the 46min-point, then turn right to the low dam. Sit on the dam wall, listen to the sound of running water and watch the fish swimming. There is some shade nearby.

8a, b THE ENCHANTED POOLS (map on page 67)

🚗 to the 29km marker, about 2km east of Planes, on the CV700 (Car tour 2); 16min or 31min on foot. (a) Follow Walk 8 (page 65) as far as the pools (16min 🛱) — or drive there on the narrow road; you may find room to park. Refresh yourself with the cool water or just sit on the steps. There is a *font* nearby and shade from the sides of the gorge. (b) For a more natural spot, continue as far as the small reservoir (31min). Shade, running water, rocks to sit on and 'English meadow' atmosphere.

10a THE EBO RIVER (map pages 70-1)

🚗 to Vall d'Ebo (the 33km point on Car tour 2); 20min on foot (or only 11min, if you drive to the cemetery). Follow Walk 10 from the 3h33min-point (page 76). Choose your spot by the river, at its best when flowing. Little shade but flat rocks, deep pools and the beautiful sound of running water. Alternatively continue up to Font Xili. Shade, stone seats, views over valley and hills and fresh, clear water from the *font*.

10b-d VALL DE LAGUAR (map on pages 70-71, photos opposite and on pages 72-73)

🚗 to Fleix (Car tour 1); 5-45min on foot. Follow Alternative walk 10 (page 73). (b) Picnic at the *lavadero*

shown opposite (5min; stone seats, font, shade) or, for more spectacular settings, also with shade: (c) descend steeply down the Mozarabic trail shown on pages 72-73, to the cave and waterfall (30min); (d) go all the way down to the floor of the Río Ebo (45min).

11a, b FINCA BIXAUCA and CASA TANCAT (map on page 78)

🚗 to the CV752 near Tàrbena (Car tours 1 and 3); 3min or 25min on foot. Follow Walk 11 (page 77). (a) At 3min the grassy area beside Finca Bixauca has terrace walls to sit on, shade if you want it and fantastic views. If you venture into the longer grass in the summer be aware of the possibility of snakes. (b) At the 9min-point, fork left and descend steeply into the valley, where an old house, surrounded by cherry trees, is an idyllic, secluded setting overlooked by rugged peaks and the high cliffs of Paso Tancat. (This is the 2h53min-point on the main walk.)

12 FONTS DE L'ALGAR (map on page 81, photo on page 23)

🚗 to Fonts de l'Algar (Car tour 1); no walking. Follow 'How to get there' at the top of Walk 12 (page 80), to park at Casa Federico. On weekdays out of season it is very quiet here, and you can sit at the side of the pools, by the little waterfalls (no shade).

13a, b FONT MOLI (map page 86) 🛱

🚗 to Guadalest (Car tour 3); no walking, or 10min on foot. Follow 'How to get there' at the top of Walk 13 (page 85), to park at Font Molí. (a) Here there is a *font* and picnic benches on two levels — but little shade. (b) For a more inspiring spot make a start on Walk 13 and at the 6min-point take the track straight ahead, to a flat shaded area

(10min). There are two rickety picnic tables, or take a blanket and sit on the ground overlooking the valley and the mountains to the north.

16 FONT DE PARTAGAT (map page 93)

🚗 to Font de Partagat (Car tour 3); no walking. This *area recreativa,* on the route of Walks 13 and 16, is in a fantastic setting, surrounded by massive cliffs and rocky outcrops. There's a font, barbecue facilities, stone benches and shade. Plenty of opportunity for strolling. Avoid busy weekends and *fiestas.*

18a BARRANC DEL SINC (map on pages 100-101, photo on page 103)

🚗 to Alcoi (Car tour 4); 8min on foot. Follow 'How to get there' at the top of Walk 18 to park near the brickworks. Then follow the walk for 8min. Delightful area beside the cobbled path and steps which lead up the *barranc.* There are rocks to sit on, and the towering cliffs provide plenty of shade. After heavy rains there will be water in the *barranc.*

18b, c SANT CRISTOFOL (map on pages 100-101) 📷

🚗 to Cocentaina (Car tour 4); no walking, or 25min on foot. (b) At the roundabout, just before leaving the town, turn left to Sant Cristófol, and drive up to this *zona recreativa* (about 1km). The large terraced complex has an attractive picnic and barbecue area as well as a *font,* some caves, a *mirador,* a bar-restaurant and plenty of shade. (c) Drive *past* the picnic site and continue up the road to a *mirador* just below Cocentaina castle. A path leads to the castle in about 10min, but for the picnic spot turn sharp right at the *mirador* and follow Alternative walk 18 (but in reverse) for 25min — to an idyllic setting under the cliff, on the top terrace of almond and olive groves.

There is shade, rocks and planks to sit on and magnificent views over to Serrella and Aitana.

19 ERMITA DE LA MARE DE DEU (map on pages 100-101) 📷

🚗 to Agres (Car tour 4) and follow signs to the *ermita* and convent; no walking. There is a bar-restaurant here, but the nearby picnic benches are in a beautiful setting, with views over the Agres valley. Shade, *font.*

20 FONT MARIOLA (map on pages 100-101) 📷

🚗 to Font Mariola (Car tour 4); no walking. See Car tour 4 at the 100km-point (page 32), to drive to the *font.* It could be busy here in season and at weekends, but otherwise this is an idyllic spot. There are benches, ample shade, a large water tank and a little *canaleta* running by.

21 FONT ROJA (map on page 114, photo on page 113) 📷

🚗 to the Parc Natural de Font Roja (optional detour at the 55km-point on Car tour 4); no walking. Extensive picnic areas in the pines, with benches, barbecue areas, water. Heavily wooded, with several signposted walks. Avoid on Sundays or in high season.

22 PENAGUILA CASTLE VIEW (map on page 116)

🚗 to El Coyao on the A171 about 3km before Penàguila (Car tour 4); 10min on foot. Follow Walk 22 from the 24min-point (page 117) as far as the crest. This rocky vantage point is in full sun, but views of the castle and surrounding mountains and valleys are breathtaking.

23a POU DEL SURDO (map on page 121, photo on page 120)

🚌 or 🚗 (Car tour 4) to Port de la Carrasqueta; 23min on foot. Follow Walk 23 (page 119) as far as the *pou.*

The 'forgotten finca' *(Picnic 25a) is worth exploring — it has a functioning well, an old* canaleta, *and (about 50m/yds behind the house) a large underground tunnel.*

There is plenty to explore, an old snow well, some shade if you want it, and fine views.

23b MAS DE LA COVA (map on page 121)

🚗 to La Sarga (Car tour 4); no walking necessary but, for the agile, there is an optional climb up to some prehistoric cave paintings. Park at Mas de la Cova (see the 136km-point on page 34). The house is uninhabited, but its fields still cultivated. A peaceful spot, some shady trees and places to sit. On the hillside, overhanging rocks shelter caves containing prehistoric paintings, and the path to them can be seen clearly from here. It is steep and narrow and it will take about 10min to negotiate.

24 RAMBLA DELS MOLINS (map on the reverse of the touring map)

🚗 to the Catí-Petrer road (see Car tour 5 after 99km; page 38); up to 20min on foot. Follow Walk 24 (page 122) from the 3h14min-point, from the restaurant down into the river bed. A particularly spectacular setting under steep sandy cliffs is reached after about

16min. Oleanders grow along the river bed, there are rocks to sit on and shade if required.

25a 'FORGOTTEN *FINCA'* (map on the reverse of the touring map, photo above)

🚗 to Castalla (Car tour 5); 50min on foot (or 35min if you drive as far as Fam, Fum y Fret). See 'How to get there' at the top of Walk 25 (page 126), then follow the Short walk to the *finca* shown below. A secluded spot overlooking the Castalla valley, with shade and plenty to explore.

25b ERMITA DE CATI (map on the reverse of the touring map)

🚗 to Xorret de Catí (see Car tour 5 after 84km; page 38); 20min on foot. From the hotel head south on the road (walkers' signpost PR-CV 29). After 2min turn left uphill on a track. Pass the large Casa de la Administración on your right, with a nearby *nevera* (9min). At a junction of tracks (15min) go right; this leads to the *ermita*. Fabulous far-reaching views over El Cid and the Serra de Maigmó. Shade in surrounding pine woods.

☀ Touring

Our five car tours cover the northern and central parts of Alicante Province. Each tour begins from one of the major tourist towns on the coast; wherever you are based, the starting point is easily accessible.

There are **three main types of road** in this part of the country. The AP7 *autopista*, or motorway, which runs north to south is the quickest way to travel between coastal towns. However, it is a toll road and quite expensive. The parallel N332 tends to become congested even outside the tourist season and progress can be slow. Some of our tours follow parts of the A31 *autovia*, the main inland road north from Alicante, and it presents few traffic problems. Other roads tend to be narrow and, in the mountains, rather winding. They carry relatively little traffic, but what traffic there is might well be travelling in the middle of the road … and going either very fast or very slowly. *Take great care at all times and expect the unexpected.* Road numbers do change; we have tried to give sufficient instructions to ensure that this causes only minor irritation.

Many of the towns or villages on the tours are well worth exploring, whether to visit their museums, study their architecture or just to absorb their atmosphere. We recommend that you **park somewhere suitable and continue on foot**, particularly through the older quarters. Streets were built to accommodate pedestrians or donkey carts, not motor vehicles; even in the smallest of cars you may find yourself in a very 'tight spot'.

Our touring notes are brief, giving only the minimum of historical detail. Instead we place emphasis on times and distances, road conditions and possibilities for sightseeing, **picnicking** and **walking**. During a long car tour you may encounter a landscape which you would like to explore at leisure another day.

The old village of Famorca rises above almond groves (Car tour 3).

Our touring times allow for no stops or detours and, of course, assume driving within the speed limit. **The pull-out touring map is designed to be held out opposite the touring notes**; **symbols** on the map correspond to those in the text. On main roads you will find that **petrol stations** are plentiful; in the mountains some of the small villages have a pump (well signposted and open during normal business hours).

When touring *do* make sure that you always carry **plenty of water**. A car can become very hot and uncomfortable in the sunshine, and there is not always a convenient bar just where you might want one. If you intend stopping en route to buy **food**, remember to do so before shops close up for their extended lunch break. All the towns and most of the villages you will pass through have bars. Those that don't provide full meals usually have a selection of *tapas* or can make up a *bocadillo*. Bars and petrol stations are likely to have toilets.

In winter it can be cold and windy in the mountains, so take adequate **warm clothing**. Whatever the time of year, **the sun can be strong**. Suncream and head covering are a must if you wander in the villages, stop for a picnic or take a stroll. Even with our long experience of Spain, we are sometimes surprised at the strength of the sun.

Allow plenty of time for the tours. You will derive little pleasure from rushing from place to place. The pace of life, especially in rural Spain, is slow, and you will do well to imitate it. Stop and explore or investigate things that catch your eye. We have found that it is often purely by chance that we stumble on something quite delightful.

Please heed the country code on page 11.

Car tour 1: COSTA BLANCA NEW AND OLD

Benidorm • Cap de la Nau • Xàbia • Cap de Sant Antoni • Dénia • Orba • Fleix • Fonts de l'Algar • Benidorm

179km/111mi; 4-5 hours' driving; exit C from Benidorm (plan page 8) On route: ⊼ at Penyal d'Ifach, Cap de Sant Antoni, Cova de les Calaveres, Fonts de l'Algar, Polop, La Nucia; Picnics (see *P* symbol and pages 10-15): 2b-d, 3, 5, 10b-d, 11, 12; Walks 1-3, 5, 10, 11, 12

If you have time for only one car tour this is the one to do. The heavily populated, affluent coastal strip is picturesque and fascinating, contrasting starkly with the landscape presented as you turn in towards the mountains. Then you are suddenly confronted with vast open spaces, layer upon layer of serras, tiny villages clinging to hillsides and picture-postcard views of mountain peaks. This is the real Costa Blanca, and we hope that it whets your appetite for exploring on foot.

Leave Benidorm from Rincón de Loix, at the eastern end of Platja de Llevant: take the northbound Avinguda del Ametlla de Mar. (To the right at this junction is the road to *P*5 and the start of Walk 5). After 3km turn right for 'PLAYA DEL ALBIR'. The road runs through orange groves, parallel to the Serra Gelada — its ridge looking quite benign from this side. Turn right again at 7km ('PLATJA DE L'ALBIR'); after about 0.5km you pass the road where Walk 5 brings you from the Serra Gelada into **Albir** (8km ✕). Continue through the town on the main road beside the beach, following 'ALTEA' signs. The Albir lighthouse stands out prominently at the end of the serra, while ahead, behind Altea church, is the flattish-topped mountain of Oltá, focus of Walk 3.

In **Altea** (10km ✝ ▲ ✕ ⊟) drive past the yacht and fishing harbours, and take the road along the seafront. Then turn left up to the parallel main road (N332) whenever you wish (it may depend on traffic). Pass palm-fringed villas hidden behind walls dripping with bougainvilleas and cross the estuary of the Algar and Guadalest rivers, before reaching a crest. Below are the moorings of a private yacht club and, ahead, the remains of Calp Castle high on a peak at the end of the Serra de Toix.

Immediately after passing through the Mascarat tunnels a closer view of Oltá presents itself ahead and soon afterwards Penyal d'Ifach comes into sight. At 22km take the turn-off right for 'CALP SUD'. (Just beyond the turn, a road goes up left to the railway station (*'estació'*), starting point for Walk 3.) Enter **Calp** (24km ☐✝ ▲ ✕ ⊟⊕) and follow the main road downhill, heading towards Penyal d'Ifach. Apart from this amazing rock (see opposite) and a couple of good beaches, Calp also has its own *salinas* — salt pools — which are just to the left of the road (25km). You will notice flamingos as you drive by, but a short stroll will also reveal many waders. At the end of the *salinas* turn right and follow signs to 'PARC NATURAL DEL PENYAL D' IFACH'. Park where you can (it may well be very busy here in the summer). Leave your car for a while and admire the views of the Serra Gelada and Calp Bay (🚏📷) — perhaps taking a short walk in these beautiful surroundings.

Return to the *salinas* and turn right, parallel to the sea. Oltá rises on your left. Just before the large 'Mercadona' supermarket (29km), a road goes right to 'Cala Calalga' (brown sign). Walk 2d (*P*2d) starts 600m down this road, not far past the Hotel Esmeralda. Stop at the *mirador* (31km 📷) for views of Cap de Moraira, Penyal d'Ifach and the coast. Pass the beach resorts of Benissa, itself situated a few kilometres inland. After cresting a rise, you return to sea level, passing promenade gardens. At the first roundabout in **Moraira** (40km ✕🍴), turn left on the CV743 for 'Teulada', curling above healthy vineyards. At a roundabout (42km) go straight on for 'BENITATXELL', noticing the antennas crowning the Cumbre del Sol on the right, before climbing into **Benitatxell** (45km).

Turn right on the CV740 for 'XÀBIA'. Pass a football ground on the right and go right again (46.5km) on a road signposted 'CANSALADES' (CV747). Go straight over a roundabout for 'XÀBIA'; the few vineyards and almond trees are mostly surrounded by scrub. Follow the road as it sweeps round past villas and the 'Salones Carrasco' on the right (51km), then go right immediately on the main Cap de la Nau road (CV742). Continue through woods and between vines and almond trees until you come to a right-hand bend where, straight ahead, a cross — the **Creu del Portitxol** — overlooks the coast. This viewpoint (55km 📷) is the starting point for *P*2c and Walk 2c to Cap Prim (in summer, parking could be difficult). Continue winding up the hill where yet more development has encroached on this once heavily wooded area. Pass a turn off

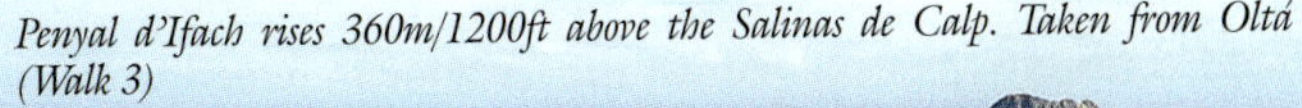

Penyal d'Ifach rises 360m/1200ft above the Salinas de Calp. Taken from Oltá (Walk 3)

right to La Granadella (57km), a secluded cove. The road becomes even more built up and descends to the lighthouse of **Cap de la Nau★** (59km ✕🎦). There are superb coastal views from the *mirador.*

Turn round and go back towards Xàbia. Views are quite different from this new perspective. The rocky mass of Montgó (photograph page 11) immediately dominates the skyline ahead, becoming ever more impressive as you draw nearer. Ignore a left turn to Benitatxell (67km) and continue to **Xàbia** (⚓▲✕🚏⊕M; Walk 2a). At the end of the dual carriageway, pass McDonald's and Lidl, then turn left at the large round-about on the Avinguda del Trenc d'Albir (71km). Keep following signs for 'DÉNIA' in the one-way system. This is the Carrer de Dénia a Xàbia (CV7361) which zigzags up and out of Xàbia. Just after you leave the town boundary you will see the Ermita de Santa Lucia (⚓) atop a hill to your left and, a little further on, an entrance to the **Parc Natural del Montgó**. Soon after-wards, turn right (74km) for 'CAP DE SANT ANTONI' (brown sign). The road takes you through pleasant wooded country-side, past villas and haciendas and, on the right, the imposing Santuario de Nuestra Señora de los Angeles (⚓; parking for P2b). A couple of kilometres further on, Walk 2b starts at the *zona recreativa* on the left (🛖). The road then crests the hill, opening up views of Cap de Sant Antoni lighthouse and over the coast to Cap de la Nau and Xàbia Bay. From the *mirador* just before **Cap de Sant Antoni★** lighthouse (78km 🎦) admire the majestic cliffs of the headland visited in Walk 2a.

Return to the Dénia road, turn right and drive around the base of Montgó. Just past the Camp de Tir (shooting range; 82km) and another entrance to the Parc Natural, the road reaches a crest from where, on a clear day, you can see all the way to Valencia and beyond, with Dénia in the foreground.

From here the road winds down into **Dénia** (🏠⚓▲△ ✕🚏⊕M; see plan on page 9). Go straight on at the roundabout and through the outer suburbs to the promenade (87km). The road continues past the part of the harbour to a large round-about behind which is the Cruz Roja (Red Cross) building. Go left at the roundabout, following 'CENTRE URBÀ'. The railway station is off to the left, a little over a block away. Follow the traffic flow to the left and then take the first right into Passeig de Saladar, a wide road mostly taken up by a palm-lined central reservation and many parked cars. Turn left at the second crossroads (Carrer de Diana), cross the railway line and go straight ahead up Camí de Sant Joan, heading for Montgó. Go straight over a roundabout, then fork right just before the Al

Khalif mosque, and turn right into Assagador de Santa Llúcia (92km; small sign for 'PARE PERE'). At a Y-fork, go left at a walkers' sign for 'RUTAS/RUTES MONTGÓ' (93km), then keep right at the next, unsigned, Y-fork. Pare Pere, a quite pretty and ornate Franciscan *ermita,* is still in use and is a popular place for visitors.

Continue past the *ermita*. Shortly you will pass, on the left, the asphalted Dénia entrance to the Parc Natural del Montgó; Walk 1 starts 100m up this road (Carrer Fenas). The road you are on winds some 800 metres (half a mile) downhill to a T-junction, where you turn left into Assagador de Cabanes (later Pou de la Muntanya); this takes you through a housing estate. Cross the railway line back into Dénia and go straight on at the next junction. At the large roundabout, take the exit past the MAPFRE building signposted 'HOSPITAL SAN CARLOS/ ALACANT/VALÈNCIA'. Keep on this road, following similar signs, past the Repsol petrol station (⛽), and go straight on at the next four roundabouts. You have now left Dénia and should take the well-signposted slip road on the right to 'LA XARA' (99km). Go left at the roundabout and into **La Xara**, where Pedreguer, your next destination, is signposted straight ahead.

Now you can relax a little and enjoy the gentle rural countryside along the CV724, old villages perched on hillsides and some spectacular mountains. Pass through groves of oranges and date palms before reaching **Pedreguer** (105km). Take the first exit from the roundabout (it may be signposted 'CUEVA') and, 0.4km further on, take care not to miss your right turn on the CV733 for 'BENIDOLEIG'. As you drive through a fertile

Scene in Tàrbena

valley, the old sturdy *fincas* make a change from white villas, and the serras ahead give you a taste of what is to come. Rounding a bend just after a shady layby (110km ⏴), come to the **Cova de les Calaveres★**, with prehistoric remains and stalactites, stalagmites and rock domes over 20m/65ft high.

In **Benidoleig** (111km) keep straight on towards Orba. Ahead is the Vall de Laguar and rising to the left the serra shown on page 1, Cavall Verd (Green Horse). Depending on which account you read, the ridge was named for its physical appearance or after a Moorish knight who used to appear there on a green horse to defend his territory. At **Orba** (115km ⬜♣✕) go past the Masymas supermarket, then turn left at the T-junction. At the roundabout 0.5km further on go right for 'La Vall de Laguar' (CV718). Wind up through olive groves and citrus orchards, with magnificent views (📷) of the surrounding serras and valleys. Keep to the CV718; then, at a junction (118km), take the left fork signposted 'La Vall de Laguar' (CV721). Notice the defile created by the Ebo River, clearly visible in the valley to the right. You soon pass the road to the Sanatorio de Fontilles, a leper colony dating from 1909. It is also a research centre. The road ascends, with stunning panoramas (📷), into the **Vall de Laguar**, through **Campell** and up to **Fleix** (122km). If you have waited till now to picnic, park at the school (just off the CV721, on the right) — the starting point for Walk 10. A few metres up the main road, where it continues to Benimaurell, take the lane off to the right. You can picnic at the *lavadero* shown on page 12 or follow the Mozarabic trail shown on pages 72-73 down to a cave, a waterfall and the valley floor (**P**10b-d).

Return through Fleix and Campell, gaining intermittent views of Orba castle perched prominently on top of a crag. At the roundabout at the entrance to Orba (128km), turn right for Benidorm (CV715; 129km ⬛). Contour around the slopes, then zigzag uphill. You will get closer views of Orba castle from here with the impressive peaks of Cavall Verd to its left. The road then descends through olive groves, crosses the Xaló River and climbs again. Just after the km15 marker, notice the isolated building, with a pine tree in front, set up on the saddle ahead to the left — the restaurant on the Coll de Rates. At **Parcent** (133km ♣✕) the road heads right towards 'Tàrbena' and winds steeply uphill. *Miradors* (📷 138km; 140.5km) give fantastic views over the valley.

From the Coll de Rates (540m/1770ft; 141km ✕) the road descends above the Barranc de Binarreal in what locals call the Tàrbena Valley. It is surrounded by astonishing serras, and on

Fonts de l'Algar

a clear day the views are breath-taking. You might see choughs cavorting over the valley as the road undulates through terraced hill-sides, giving a fresh view at every turn. Pass the CV752 off right (148km) to the start of Walk 11 and *P*11 and continue into **Tàrbena** (149km ✕). Then wind down to another *mirador* (152km 📷), from where you can see Bolulla Castle stuck on its crag (▯) ... and down to Benidorm. Alternative walk 12-2 starts and ends at this viewpoint.

Continue to descend steeply, passing sheer crags and deep gorges, the most impressive being the Paso Tancat, to **Bolulla** (156km). As you leave the village, Penya Severino, the culmination of the Bernia Ridge, dominates the view to the left and does so all the way down to the Algar Valley. Blessed with a great deal of underground water, this valley is one of the most fertile in the area.

Turn right (159km) on the slip road signposted to 'FONTS DE L'ALGAR' and follow similar signposting from the round-about. Descend through a sea of plastic greenhouses to **Fonts de l'Algar★** (**✕⛩△M**) and, a little over 1km downhill, look for the restaurant Casa Federico on the left: out of season you will be able to use its car park, which is just alongside some attractive pools (*P*12). Walk 12 starts here. In high season, continue uphill to one of the paid car parks. The complex, with waterfalls, *fonts* and other attractions, is worth exploring.

Return to the main road and continue into **Callosa d'En Sarrià** (165km ✝▲✕⛽⊕M). At the roundabout in the centre take the third exit, for 'BENIDORM' (still the CV715). Cross the Guadalest River (167km) and soon Campana comes into view, towering ahead of you. Drive through **Polop** (169km), past gardens (⛩) on the right. You might like to stop briefly in Polop to look at its fountain which has 221 spouts (yes, really) and is decorated with tiles representing the shields of all the administrative areas of Alicante. Continue along a crescent-shaped 'esplanade' road into **La Nucia** (170km). Leaving La Nucia (⛩), the Serra Gelada again looms into view. Pass a road off right to Finestrat (177km) and follow the road all the way back into Benidorm (179km), then use the plan (page 8) or your smartphone to find the best route back to your hotel.

Car tour 2: NORTHERN VALLEYS — THE CHERRY ROUTE

Dénia • Pego • Planes de la Baronía • Beniarrés • L'Orxa • Vall de Gallinera • L'Atzubia • Dénia

120km/74mi; just over 3 hours' driving; exit A
On route: ⛱ *at the limekilns, Alcalà, L'Orxa; Picnics (see* **P** *symbol and pages 10-15): 6, 8, 10a; Walks 6-9*

Some motorists may find the sheer drops on several stretches unnerving. Fill up with petrol at Pego; it's not available anywhere in the mountains.

This tour is probably the most scenic in the area. It follows the northern valleys where every available plot of land is cultivated. While orange, almond and olive trees abound, the abundant cherry trees leave the most lasting impression. The area is particularly attractive after spring rains, when it is lusciously green, and the trees are in full blossom. You will have spectacular views of surrounding serras, including the unusual horned peaks of the Serra de Benicadell. Enjoy them, but take care on the many bends in the narrow valley roads.

Leave Dénia by Exit A (the C725, signposted to the motorway and 'ALACANT'). At a major junction outside **Ondara** (9km), keep in the left lane for 'CV332/ONDARA/VALENCIA' (white sign), *not* the right lane (blue motorway sign). *Carefully* keep to the N332 until you can take the signposted exit for 'EL VERGER/PEGO' (CV700). Then ignore the slip road for El Verger, take the *next* exit for 'PEGO', eventually passing under the motorway. Soon Pego is directly ahead, nestling at the foot of the mountains, its church prominent against the hillside. It is an important town and might well be called the 'gateway to the mountains'. At the third roundabout in **Pego** (20km ⬜✝▲ ✕⛽⊕), turn left on the CV715, following signs for 'SAGRA/ CALLOSA' and passing the tourist office on the left. Following the convoluted turns of the C715, watch for the KM10 marker and, just beyond it (21km) turn right on the CV712 for Vall d'Ebo, winding steeply up a road through pine woods. After about 5km there are magnificent views (📷) over Pego deep in the valley, overlooked by its castle high on a hill. You are right in the heart of the mountains, enjoying spectacular scenery.

After rounding the hillsides, the road climbs to a pass (29km), with an old converted windmill on the right. Just over the crest a deep gorge, the Barranc del Infern, cuts through the barren mountains (📷). Descend through market gardens and orchards. On the approach to Vall d'Ebo you cross a blue-painted bridge (33km). About 30m straight ahead there is a road to the left where you could park, to take a stroll along the river (**P**10a). But the tour turns right just over the bridge for 'COVA DEL RULL' (brown sign) and bypasses Vall d'Ebo (✝✕⊕△), following the river.

Turn right across another bridge and drive out of the valley, past a huge cave, the **Cova del Rull**★ (∩ 36km). Soon the natural rock arch at the end of the Serra de Foradá comes into sight ahead. Then, in a sheltered spot just before another bridge, you encounter the first of the many cherry orchards. Cross the high plateau, the road lined in places with sage, rosemary and thyme (sorry, no parsley!) and the air alive with flocks of goldfinch. Make a stop at 43km to visit the ancient limekilns (☗) and a *nevera* (snow well), then continue past **Alcalà de la Jovada** (44km ☗Δ). Both Vall d'Ebo and Alcalà have vastly reduced populations now, but originally formed an important part of the territory of the legendary Moorish ruler known as Al Azraq. This cherry route was all part of his 13th-century 'kingdom', and many of the terraced lands you see owe their structure to the Moors he ruled.

Pass by the village of **Margarida** (☐✗), then turn left for 'PLANES' (50km) on the Vall de Gallinera road (CV700), passing the Venta de Margarida. Just after crossing the Pont de les Calderes (53km), a narrow road leads to the Barranc de la Encantada (Walk 8). Why not park on the left about 100m past the bridge and take a walk along the *barranc* (**P**8)? Continue towards Planes, overlooked by the Ermita del Santo Cristo. Planes (☐✝✗Δ) is worth a detour to see its setting around the medieval castle and old aqueduct which still serves the wash-house.

But the main tour bypasses Planes: just before reaching the village, turn right for 'BENIARRÉS' (54km). This little road (C711) descends steeply into the valley. As you climb out the other side, notice first a lane and then steps on the right to the Santo Cristo *ermita* (✝) high above. On the left catch sight of a reservoir and the little white church at Beniarrés standing prominently on top of a hill, with Benicadell rising majestically behind it (photo on page 66). The road descends to the **Presa de Beniarrés** (also called Embassament de Beniarrés), where we have seen osprey, herons, cormorants, ducks and other waterbirds. Cross the dam (60km) and continue round the other side. When you reach the junction with the CV701/CV705 just before Beniarrés (64km), turn right for 'CASTELLO/L'ORXA'; then turn right again on the CV701 for 'L'ORXA' and drive past Beniarrés (✝) following the wide valley of the river Serpis. The valley, heavily wooded and cultivated (more cherries), is green throughout the year and the high mountain ahead of you is La Safor, climbed in Walk 7.

Just as you approach a bridge over the river Serpis, a road on your left leads 0.5km uphill to the old railway station shown on

PERPUTXENT CASTLE
This impressive fortress, setting for Picnic 6, was initially the stronghold of Al Azraq before being reconquered by Jaime I. It subsequently came into the hands of the Knights Templar, was confiscated and came under the power of Jaime II. It then passed to the new Orden Militar de Santa María de Montesa.

page 63, starting point for Walk 6 through the Serpis Valley. Cross the bridge and turn right (71km) into **L'Orxa** (72km ▯⊼), at the end of the Serpis Gorge and protected by the Castell de Perputxent (*P*6; photo at the left). Walk 7 starts at Font Grota (⊼), at the entrance to the village, in a garden on your right. Drive past the village, alongside the dry river bed. When you come to a T-junction, turn left (small white sign: 'VILLALONGA/ LLACUNA'). You wind steeply up to the ridge behind L'Orxa on a narrow but well-surfaced road, with fine views of Benicadell off to the right (photo on page 4). Drive past terraces all the way to the top, then head across the flat-topped ridge to a T-junction and a STOP sign (78km). Turn right, and descend towards the Serra de Foradá on a road which is often only one lane wide.

Very tight hairpin bends take you into the **Vall de Gallinera**. Cross a (usually dry) ford and turn left into **Alpatró** (82km). Here you rejoin the CV700, turning left towards 'PEGO'. Almond and orange orchards grace the terraces, but soon it becomes evident that each little village derives its living from the abundant cherry trees. In spring you'll be surrounded by the beauty and fragrance of the blossom; in summer you can buy the fruit. The road runs high above the *barranc* and there are some fantastic views down the Gallinera Valley (83km ⊡). You pass through the little settlements of **La Carroja** (✕), **Benis-sivá** and **Benialí**. The turret of Gallinera Castle (Walk 9, photo on page 69) comes into view on top of a hill ahead, and steep cliffs close in on either side as you leave the valley. The countryside eventually opens out again into terraced orchards surrounding **L'Atzubia** (97km), where Walk 9 begins, and Pego comes into view straight ahead. From **Pego** (101km), follow signs for Dénia, bypassing the centre and retracing your outgoing route back to Dénia (120km).

Calp • Callosa d'En Sarrià • Guadalest • Confrides • Gorga • Castell de Castells • Xaló/Jalón • Calp

135km/84mi; 3-4 hours' driving from Calp
On route: ⻌ at Callosa, Confrides, Quatretondeta, Castell de Castells;

Picnics (see *P* symbol and pages 10-15): 11, 13, 15, 16; Walks 3, 11, 13, 15, 16

Mountains surround you on the outward route through the picturesque Guadalest Valley and on the return along a narrow, winding road through the Jalón Valley. Almond groves are a major feature of the landscape: in January and February large areas are ablaze with pink and white blossom. But at any time, the variety of scenery provided by the two valleys with their surrounding serras makes this tour unforgettable.

Leave Calp (Walk 3) from the Plaça Central. Drive up the hill on the dual carriageway, following signs to 'ALICANTE'. Stay in the left lane, and at the top take the underpass towards 'ALICANTE', to join the N332 going south. Every bit of land has been developed for housing. Calp Castle is prominent as you continue under the railway line, down into the Mascarat Gorge and through three tunnels cut from the sheer rock of the mountainside. Turn right off the CV332 for 'CALLOSA D'EN SARRIÀ' (9km); then, just under 1km along, turn right again for 'CALLOSA' and go under the AP7 motorway (10km).

You are now on the CV755 and almost immediately going through **Altea la Vella**, an upmarket residential area situated just under the Bernia Ridge. Take in the amazing views of Campana, Ponoch and the Serra de Aitana, ahead and to the left, as you drive through seemingly endless citrus groves. In stark contrast to the barren mountains, the countryside stretching out at either side of the road is lush and green. As well as the more common fruit and nut trees there are large groves of *nísperos* (medlars), easily distinguished by their much denser and darker foliage.

At the roundabout in the centre of **Callosa d'En Sarrià** (19km ✝⛰✕⛽⊕M) take the third exit to 'ALCOI' and 'GUADALEST'. The road (⻌) skirts high above the Riu Guadalest with fantastic views encompassing the valley and Guadalest Castle. Just before crossing the river (✕ and **M** of old cars and motorcycles) the serras of Aixorta and Serrella dominate the landscape as the road winds quite steeply uphill. On rounding the bend, just after a bar with a commanding view of the valley, enjoy your first close-up of the remains of Guadalest Castle perched on top of its rocky outcrop. Further round, houses come into view, clinging precariously to the slopes below the castle. As you pass a rather grand drystone wall and a *mirador*

(28km 📷), the buttresses of Penya Mulero (Walk 13), much favoured by golden eagles, rise on the left.

Pass a road off to the right (30km) to the Presa de Guadalest; it leads to the start of Walk 15. **Guadalest**★ (31km ⌂✕M📷) is a one-street village of scarcely 200 inhabitants. But in summer it is bristling with tourists on account of its superb setting. The rocks rise up alongside the road and the *mirador* (📷) at the castle affords a magnificent panorama of the surrounding serras. As you drive through the village you enjoy a first view of Benifató Castle in the distance. At a roundabout under 1km outside Guadalest go straight on (CV70 for Alcoi), almost immediately passing a turn-off left to El Trestellador restaurant (33km); Walk 13 starts about 1.5km up this road (*P*13).

Pass through **Benimantell** (✕) and climb up past Restaurante Venta de Benifató to a junction (36km). Turn sharp left at a village sign for **Benifató** (⌂) and somewhat under 0.5km further on, at another village sign for Benifató turn sharp right ('Font de Partagat' is a tiled sign on a wall at the left). This narrow and winding road heads up towards the buttresses of Partagat. Pass the little road where Walk 16 comes in from the right and reach **Font de Partagat** (40km; *P*16). Walk 16 heads upwards from here but, for the car tour, return the same way after you have explored a bit.

Once back at the CV70, turn left to **Confrides** (49km ✝♠✕). From here the road climbs past an isolated shop called 'El Rincón de las Mermeladas', selling local cheeses, preserves, etc, and through a pass (966m; 53km 📷), before descending into the next valley. The hills ahead, being less rocky, are more gentle, and there are many paths ribboning up the slopes which are wooded or terraced almost to the tops.

Continue through **Benasau** (60km ✝✕). Cocentaina Castle (⌂) stands out on the stark hillside ahead just before you turn right on the CV710 (63km) for 'GORGA'. This road undulates through pretty rural countryside to **Gorga** (67km), where it takes a sharp right turn at the roundabout towards 'QUATRE-TONDETA' (CV754). You are now heading eastwards again on the northern side of the Serra de Serrella; the soft rock makes for some unusual formations. Drive across several bridges which span a series of shallow gorges before winding uphill to the right of **Quatretondeta** (72km ♠✕🏠).

As the narrow road contours round the slopes watch for small birds. Some will only be summer visitors, but the chirpy serins with their yellow flashes abound in the fruit trees all year. When you join the CV720 at **Facheca**, a little village tucked into the hillside (77km), turn right and pass the old village of

Bell-tower at Guadalest

Famorca (80km). The road, now wider but still winding, crosses more dry river beds. The spectacular Serra de Aixorta becomes visible ahead, with Serrella Castle on a peak to its right (85km 📷). Wind gradually downhill towards picturesque **Castell de Castells** (88km ⚑▲✕), nestling in the valley below. Just before crossing the bridge and entering the village, turn right towards 'TARBENA'. Park by the picnic tables (⊓) if you wish to explore the village, a maze of narrow streets.

Then continue along the winding CV752. Just past the KM3 road marker (97km) a road to the right marks the start of Walk 11 (**P**11). The long ridge of Ferrer and the rugged peaks of Bernia rise on the left. On the outskirts of **Tàrbena** (100km ✕) turn left on the CV715 (signed to 'ORBA' and 'PEGO'). The road affords views into the Binarreal Valley (Walk 12) as it contours to the Coll de Rates (540m/1770ft; 107km ✕). Wind down into the Jalón Valley, past two viewpoints (📷 107.5km, 110km), towards **Parcent** (114km ⚑✕). Just inside this village, which is dominated by its church, turn right on the CV720 for 'ALCALALÍ'. Almond groves lead the eye to the Serra del Cavall Verd (photo on page 1). Just after entering **Alcalalí** (117km ✕), ignore a right turn towards 'Centro Urbano', but then turn right towards 'XALO' just 100m further on (CV750).

Xaló/Jalón★ (120km ⚑▲✕🍴) is very much given over to expatriates and tourists. Many of the streets (and the dry river bed) are lined with flea-market stalls on Saturdays; restaurants and *bodegas* abound. As the road bears right, avoiding the centre, look up the little streets to the left and catch glimpses of the old town and blue dome of the small church. Climb out of the valley, through some vineyards, cross over the motorway, and turn right on the N332 for 'CALP'. As you descend through more vineyards, flat-topped Oltá (Walk 3) and the rugged Bernia Ridge become prominent on the right, and the Penyal d'Ifach (shown on page 19) comes into view ahead. Take the left turn to 'CALP NORTE' (134km 🍴), back to the Plaça Central (135km).

Car tour 4: SOUTHERN VALLEYS AND WESTERN HIGHLANDS

Benidorm • Sella • Penàguila • Alcoi • Cocentaina • Bocairent • Coves de Canalobre • Benidorm

216km/134mi; 5 hours' driving; exit A from Benidorm (plan page 8)
On route: ⌂ at Penàguila, Font Roja, Cocentaina; Picnics (see *P* symbol and pages 10-15): 18a-c, 19-22, 23a, 23b; Walks 4, 14, 17-23

From fertile valleys and heavily wooded hillsides to desert wastes and stark peaks — this tour takes you through all manner of landscapes. Castles, caves and prehistoric paintings are just some of the features en route, and there are frequent opportunities to leave your car. Apart from exploring the interesting settlements it takes you through, we suggest several short strolls to the features of interest. To do and see everything would be too much for one day, so consider taking two days for this tour.

Take exit A from Benidorm, heading west from the city towards Alicante. Just 3km from the junction of Armada Española and Jaume I (see plan on page 8), turn right a the roundabout towards the LEROY MERLIN, where the tour begins. From here continue on the CV767, making straight for the hills — the Cortina Ridge, with the notch of Campana standing out prominently behind it. Pass **Finestrat** (5km ✕), its houses perched precariously on a hillside, and circle clockwise to a minor crossroads, then turn left at the roundabout towards Sella on the CV758. (A right turn would take you to the parking for Walk 4.) This road climbs below Campana, affording good views of the 'shark's teeth' of El Realet. Benidorm is soon forgotten, as high-rise blocks and fancy villas give way to spectacular mountain peaks and grand old *fincas*.

At the T-junction with the C770 (13km) turn right and head towards Penya Sella — a long flat ridge ending with three peaks on the right. Climb steeply above a *barranc* and terracing and go through **Sella** (17km ✕), noticing the contrast in vegetation on the slopes either side — barren old almond terraces on the right-hand (sunny) side and dense woods on the left. Just as the road sweeps left (23km), notice a narrow uphill road on the right with very discrete yellow/white PR stripes on a rock on the right. Walk 14 which traverses the Penya Sella Ridge starts 6.5km up this road. Continuing on the CV770 as it climbs steeply, ignore a left turn to Relleu. The antennas up on the right signal Aitana — Alicante's highest mountain. At the **Port de Tudons** (27km) go left for 'PENÀGUILA' on CV785. The road passes the entrance to the Aitana Safari Park★ (28km), then climbs high above the valley. An eye-catching panorama spreads before you. Then the road levels out.

Now gradually descending the far side of the hill, you pass through heavily wooded terrain, which continues until the next valley opens out. On the far side of the rocky crag ahead are the remains of Penàguila Castle (Walk 22). Pass the gates of El Coyao on the left (37km *P*22; Short walk 22). From this point the road winds down into **Penàguila** (41km ☐♠✗🛱) and then bears left towards Benifallím. On the next sharp right-hand bend, it is worth stopping to look behind you, where the the view of the castle and a natural rock arch (the Arco de Santa Llúcia) will long remain in your memory.

Further along you pass a shuttered-up *hostal* with adjacent tower and *ermita* on the right (43km ♠). As you round another bend, Benifallím comes spectacularly into view, its castle on the left. Go past the village (45km) and follow the road towards 'ALCOI'. It undulates through pleasant scenery to a T-junction at a bridge (52km ✗), where you turn right on the N340. In the background, the Barranc del Sinc slices through the rocky cliff face.

At a roundabout just inside **Alcoi★** (55km ♠▲✗🛒⊕ M🖼), you can take an optional 18km return detour to the Santuario de la Font Roja★ (♠✗🛱△*P*21): take the third exit from the roundabout (signposted). This natural park, high in the mountains, is the setting for Walk 21 and well worth a visit. The main tour goes straight on at the roundabout, following the one-way system and signs to 'CENTRE URBÀ' and eventually 'VALENCIA' on the N340, winding all the way through Alcoi. This fascinating town, below the sheer cliffs of the Barranc del Sinc, has two centres, connected by huge bridges. You will surely want to delve into its history and explore its older quarters. Eventually you find yourself on the tree-lined Avinguda l'Alameda, where you will cross a bridge over the Barranc del Sinc (58km). Just *before* the bridge, the Economy supermarket on the right is the starting point for Walk 18. But motorists can drive much closer to the fabulous setting shown on page 103 (*P*18a) by following the *walking notes* on page 101.

Continue over the bridge and, on leaving Alcoi, you will see Cocentaina Castle prominent ahead on its rocky pinnacle; Montcabrer (Walk 18), the main peak of the Serra de Mariola rises majestically on the left. Drive through **Cocentaina** (63km ♠▲✗🛒⊕🛱) and, at the roundabout with a large sculpture just before leaving the town, notice a road going left to the castle (☐) and the Sant Cristófol *zona recreativa* (✗🛱*P*18b-c).

Some 6km from Cocentaina take the slip road signposted to 'MURO/AGRES' (CV700); then, at the roundabout, turn left towards Agres and cross the pine-clad slopes of the Agres Valley.

After going under the railway (75km), climb gradually until Agres comes into view on the left. Above the village, clinging to the hillside, is the Ermita de la Mare de Deu (*P*19) which Walk 19 passes on its way to a refuge and *cavas* (snow wells). Ignore the first signposted left turn up to the village but, just 0.45km further on, turn sharp left (76km) and drive up to **Agres** (77km ✝🔺✕). Turn left at the fork and wind up through the narrow streets of this interesting village. Continuing straight on at the crossroads (78km) would take you up Carrer Major to the church where Walk 19 starts, but the tour turns *right* into Carrer Sant Antoni. Pass Pensión Mariola and, at the end of the street (at the railings) turn sharp right and head back down to the main CV700. Turn left and continue west. As the road descends gently, look up to the left and see if you can spot Cava Gran, a circular stone building on top of the ridge; it is visited on Walk 19.

Drive through **Alfafara** (82km) passing two old *fincas* on the right, their terraced fields still well cultivated. Turn left at the T-junction (86km) signposted to 'VILLENA' (CV81), and soon have magnificent views of the old town of **Bocairent★** (✝🔺✕🚏⊕M📷), with its *ermita* high on a hill to the right. The town, shown opposite, is worth exploring: turn right (88km) at a roundabout, following 'BOCAIRENT', and go over a bridge immediately. Follow the one-way system and signs to museums and tourist office. You climb high into the village, to the large oval Plaça de l'Ajuntament (89km), housing the tourist office and museum. From here you can walk along a lane to the Covetes de los Moros★, described and illustrated on page 98. Short walk 17 will take you there, while the main walk (illustrated on page 96) goes along an old mule trail to Ontinyent. Both walks begin at the tourist office.

From the square, make your way back to the CV81 and, after crossing the bridge, turn right (🚏). Go straight on at two round-abouts for 'VILLENA', edging an industrial estate; then, at a third roundabout, go left *into* the estate for 'ALCOI' and the CV794, but immediately turn right on the CV794. Keep following the CV794 for 'ALCOI' … as this industrial estate grows ever larger. The CV794 road winds high above the Agres Valley on to a wooded plateau. Across the plateau the land opens out and several small farmhouses lie amongst the cultivated fields. After entering the woods once more, Mariola Castle appears ahead on a rocky peak. Just past the KM9 road marker you pass the entrance to a commercial campsite (100km △).

Beyond a small bridge, an unsurfaced road up to the left leads to the Font de Mariola *area recreativa*. If you would like a break, turn up here and park near the building which serves as a shelter for campers and picnickers. This is Font Mariola's free camping area, with picnic benches and a *font* (△⌐*P*20). Walk 20, to Alt de la Cova, begins here and, just past the benches, Short walk 20-2 leads up a track through pines to Mariola Castle. Returning to the road, turn left and after a few kilometres wind down across a narrow bridge. On reaching a crest, look ahead to the thickly-wooded slopes: you can see the Font Roja sanctuary. To the left and slightly lower down is Barxell Castle.

Wind down into **El Barxell** (109km) and, at the junction, turn right across the bridge towards 'BANYERES' (CV795). Within 300m pass a dirt road off to the left to Barxell Castle, a five minute walk away. The road continues across the plain, through well-cultivated farmlands and past El Altet, another old *finca* on the right. Turn left towards 'IBI' on the CV801 (116km) and climb through fertile terraces, ignoring a right turn to Onil. This Castalla/Onil/Ibi area makes almost all

Bocairent

the toys and dolls for the whole of Spain. From a crest, Ibi can be seen sprawled out in the valley below. The two hills north of the town used to bear castles, but now there are two *ermitas*, one dedicated to Santa Lucia, the other to San Miguel.

Winding downhill you have a good view of the pointed peak of Maigmó ahead. As you approach the factory at the entrance to **Ibi** (125km ♦✕➌), notice the two brick gate-posts on the left and a PR signpost. Walk 21 to Font Roja passes through here. Continue into town and, just before reaching the *ajuntament* (town hall, where Walk 21 begins), notice a street to the right: Calle Vicente Pascual. A little way along the street there is an interesting modern fountain — worth a quick visit. Set into its walls are ceramic tiles each bearing a picture — a shield or crest, a castle or *ermita*, all with some connection with Ibi.

Continue by turning left at the *ajuntament* on the CV806 and go straight on at the roundabout by the petrol station (➌) for 'ALCOI'. After passing large expanses of cultivated fields, reach another roundabout. Follow the blue signs for 'A7/ALCOI' and do the same at a second roundabout. You are now on the A7 *autovía*. Take the first exit (453) to 'XIXONA' (135km) and join the CV800 south. This road crosses a high pass, and signs will tell you if it is open. But first, shortly after turning right, take the CV786 road to the left, signposted to 'La Sarga'. Drive about 0.5km through apple orchards to the hamlet of **La Sarga**, then leave it on the right: take the *camino rural* (136km), which soon sweeps left over a *barranc* and winds up to Mas de la Cova (*P*23b). Ahead in the rock face, just a short walk away, are caves with prehistoric paintings.

Return to the main road, turn left, and wind up to the **Port de la Carrasqueta**, a pass at 1020m/3350ft. Park at the *mirador* (144km 📷) and take in the surrounding views. Walk 23 to Pou del Surdo (*P*23a; photo on page 119) and the Carrasqueta Ridge starts here. Over the pass the road winds down through steep hairpins, with ample places to pull over and take in yet more stunning views (📷). On the downhill stretch (several ✕), you pass an *ermita* (155km) and soon see the distinctive split peak of Penya Roja which towers over Xixona.

The CV800 bypasses the town, but drive into **Xixona** (157km ♦▲✕➌⊕M), the confectionery capital of Spain. Its situation in the centre of the almond-growing region determines its importance in the *turrón* (nougat) industry — it even has a museum of *turrón*! Unless you wish to explore the town, turn left in the centre for 'ALACANT' and continue through the barren waste that the landscape around Xixona has become after years of drought. Occasional sproutings of vegetation in the dry river beds give evidence of some underground water — oases in what is otherwise essentially desert. About 3km south of Xixona (161km), turn left on the CV774 for 'BUSOT'. This road snakes downhill, crosses a bridge over a dry river bed and later, near the KM3 marker, winds up to a housing development where a pair of reservoirs — one of them totally dry — comes as a surprise (169km)

Shortly after this, turn left uphill (170km) towards the Serra del Cabeço d'Or (signed 'CUEVAS DE CANALOBRE'). Situated at over 700m/2300ft, the **Coves de Canalobre★** (175km **M**), with magnificent stalactites and stalagmites, are considered the most important in the Valencian region. They were used originally for cold storage, but in the Spanish Civil War served as an arms depot. Even if you do not visit the caves, take a few minutes to admire the spectacular view (📷) over the valley.

From the caves return to the CV774 road, turn left (180km) and follow 'CENTRO URBANO' to drive through **Busot** (182km). At the main junction in the village, with a church at the left, turn left for 'AIGÜES' (CV773) and climb through yet more hairpins round the rocky mountainside, before descending to the next junction (188km), where you turn left for 'AIGÜES' on the CV775. You pass an *area recreativa* just before **Aigües de Busot** (191km **🏨✕M**), a spa town, busy at weekends. Follow signs for 'RELLEU', but after 2km (193km) turn right (*not signposted,* but the white wall of Finca Bilou is to the right, and rubbish containers/post boxes to the left).

This delightful narrow road undulates straight towards Campana, with the antennas of Aitana high on the left. At every turn and crest new beauties of nature come into focus; then the man-made **Embalse del Amadorio** appears on the left (202km). Unfortunately, you can no longer keep straight on here to cross the dam wall; the road is closed. So turn sharp left. You cross an arm of the reservoir and join the CV770 (204km), soon passing a splendid *mirador*. This road takes you over the A7 motorway and to a roundabout at the edge of **La Vila Joiosa** (✝🏨✕⛽⊕Δ). Go right for 'ALACANT', and at the next roundabout take the third exit for 'Benidorm'. Now on the N332, drive straight back into Benidorm (216km).

Alicante • Monforte del Cid • Castalla • Catí • Alicante

144km/89mi; 3 hours' driving. Exit A from Alicante (plan page 9). From elsewhere, join the tour at the A7 junction, just east of the A31. Approaching Elda, use the large-scale map on the reverse of *the touring map for help with navigation if you are going to one of the walks.* *On route: ☕ at Novelda; Picnics (see P symbol and pages 10-15): 24, 25a, 25b; Walks: 24, 25, 26*

The province of Alicante played an important role in the history of the region during the seven or eight centuries of the Reconquest from the Moors. This role can be appreciated as you consider the vast number of castles which remain today, some in ruins, others well preserved or restored. One of the best known figures associated with the period must be El Cid, the legendary 11th-century mercenary considered at the time to be a national patriot. The town and the mountain named after him feature prominently on this tour.

From the roundabout at the RENFE railway station, head west on Avinguda Aguilera (see plan on page 9), driving towards the stark mounds of the Serra de Fontcalent. Continue past the A70 junction (4km ☕) and after 1km join the A31 to Madrid (☕ 16km). Beyond the Portitxol Pass (☕ 20km) and shortly after another petrol station (☕), take the slip road to **Monforte del Cid** (22km ☐✝☕). This town, said to be one of the two oldest settlements in the province, merits a visit. A church with a striking blue ceramic dome now stands on the old fortifications, its bell tower fashioned from one of the ancient defensive towers.

Make your way back to the A31, then take Exit 213 ('NOVELDA NORTE') and head south on the N325 to **Novelda** (27km ☐✝M). Its main products are table grapes and saffron, but its main attraction is its castle. After crossing the river turn right on the CV832, signed to 'CASTILLO/CASTELL' (pink sign). After about 4km this road leads to the **Castillo de la Mola**, a national monument. There is ample parking space (37km). As you approached it was probably not the castle, but the impressive **Santuario de la Magdalena** which caught your eye. It is ornately arabesque and dates from 1912. You will have noticed picnic benches (☕) below the car park, but a better place to relax is at the top of the hill behind the sanctuary, where more benches afford a magnificent view over Aspe and Novelda.

Return to the A31 the way you came and contuine heading towards 'MADRID'. Behind the pointed hill on your right, you have your first view of the impressive El Cid, its twin peaks joined by a long shallow plateau. This view improves as you drive through the still-barren terrain, taking Exit 201 for 'ELDA HOSPITAL'. Circle the roundabout and take the first exit for

'Hospital' (CV835). Cross over the motorway, then drive along to the right of it until you can bear right for 'SAX' at a roundabout. At the T-junction with the CV833, go left into **Elda** (52km [icons]) for Walk 24 which starts at Elda station. The large town of Elda has a chequered past. In 1304 it passed from the kingdom of Castilla to that of Valencia and, after the expulsion of the Muslims in 1609, it was left deserted. Castellanos eventually repopulated the area, imposing their (Spanish) language, despite the fact that all around — even one street away in Petrer — the people spoke Valenciano.

The main tour turns right for 'SAX' at the T-junction with the CV833. Continue beside the Viñalopó Valley to **Sax** (65km [icon]). Its name derives from the Latin *saxum*, meaning large boulder. Turn right at the first roundabout, go straight on at the second roundabout and drive through the town on the CV830, round the right-hand side of the castle which sits on this 500m/1650ft-high boulder. It was built first by the Romans; rebuilt by the Arabs in the eighth century, it has one Roman and one Arabic tower. When you come to traffic lights at the right turn for Villena, you could first turn left for 'ECOPARQUE', drive round the back of the castle, park beside a gate and enter the grounds on foot. A short walk here offers a good view of the surrounding countryside, cultivated with almonds and olives.

Leaving the castle behind, return and follow 'VILLENA', crossing a bridge. At the roundabout (where you cross the railway and then the A31 *autovía*), go straight on for Castalla (CV830), joining the CV80 *autovía* signposted to 'IBI'. On the left you will see the antennas on top of Penya Rossa and the flat-topped ridge of the Serra del Frare (Walk 26); to the right is the Serra de l'Arguenya. Continue to Exit 10 for 'CASTALLA' and 'BIAR' (76km). At the top of the slip road, go straight on at the roundabout for 'CASTALLA' (CV811). (Walk 26 starts 8km up the road to the left here, in Biar.) The first town you see to the left is Onil, but then Castalla Castle appears on the right, the view becoming ever more magnificent as you draw nearer. Drive round its base to **Castalla** (82km [icons]). The town's name derives from the Latin *castra alta* or high castle, for obvious reasons. It has not been completely restored, but is worth a visit. The town also has a baroque church dating from 1613, an *ermita* and an 18th-century convent. Go straight ahead at the traffic lights, passing the church on your right. About 0.5km past the church, opposite a two-storey red brick building ('Muebles'), turn right on Manuel de Falla. Turn right at the T-junction, take the first left on Dr Fleming then (three blocks further on) go left again on Av de Petrer, heading towards the crags of Despeñador. Keep straight on to a Y-fork with a cross in the middle, where you go left on the 'CAMI DE CATÍ' (84km); 300m to the *right* at this fork is the starting point for Walk 25 (**P**25a), a long, varied hike which takes in the summit of Despeñador.

You drive through extensive almond and olive groves towards the hills, then wind up steeply through pines until you are directly under Despeñador. The road takes you round to the left and up to a crest. The twin peaks of El Cid stand out ahead as you descend into the valley, where a hotel, Xorret de Catí is visible below. Pass the **Xorret de Catí** hotel tennis courts and stop at the front entrance. You can enjoy the hotel facilities (✘▲) or stretch your legs. Alternative walk 25-3 starts here, and a walkers' signpost for the PR-CV 29 points the way to the Ermita de Catí (**P**25b).

Continue from the hotel entrance; the road curves left past the car park. Go straight on at a 'Stop' sign. You soon rise out of a dip with a view of the Pantanet Gorge off to the right (Walk 25). Pass Casa Pantanet and, at a junction (97km), turn right. (A left turn would take you to the foot of El Cid.) Continue the descent and, after a little more than 1km, look for a drystone wall on the left. This surrounds an old two-tier *era* (threshing floor), with its cylindrical millstone still in place. Shortly after this (99km) you see the beginnings of La Rambla dels Molins on the left, the watercourse on the route of Walks 24 and 25. Follow this past Restaurante Molino la Roja (✘ start of Short walk 24-1, **P**24), then drive high above the *rambla,* taking in its spectacular rock formations.

As you round a bend, Petrer Castle comes into sight. The tiny Carrer de las Casitas ('Street of the Little Houses') leading up to this Arabic castle is picturesque, and the castle itself is almost fully restored. Stop at the *mirador* (103km 📷) for a longer look; notice, too, the twin towns of Elda and Petrer and more views of El Cid. Wind downhill and, if you want to explore another town, go under the A31 *autovía,* past the Carrefour hypermarket and into **Petrer** (■✝▲✘🚌⊕). Otherwise, fork right for 'ALACANT/ALICANTE' to join the motorway. Eventually you pass the A7 junction (138km) and follow signs to the centre of Alicante and the station roundabout (144km).

Walking

While the car tours take you through spectacular countryside, it is really only when walking that you can fully appreciate the beauty of this landscape. From a car you would not notice the fish swimming contentedly in the clear and sparkling water of a mountain stream, the clump of orchids at the side of a path, the relentless call of the corn bunting or the sweet smell of rosemary. We hope that what you do see on your car tours will entice you to walk. *There are walks here for everyone to enjoy.*

As you will notice from any high vantage point, the mountains in the Costa Blanca region are criss-crossed by a myriad of tracks and paths. Some of these, used for centuries by farmers and shepherds, connect remote settlements and villages and provide access to *fincas, fonts* and fields. Others are more recent, sometimes the result of quarrying and forestry activities. The replacement of donkey and mule by tractor and trailer has resulted in many paths being widened into tracks and, in some cases, roads.

The area is well walked, and there are some classic routes, parts of which we have included. But we have, for example, rejected or adapted those which involve nothing more than a sheer slog to the summit of a mountain and back down again. In an attempt to tailor our walks specifically for users of *Landscapes* books, and taking into account the region's limited public transport service, we have tried to provide circular, rather than out-and-back walks. In order to make this possible we sometimes include short stretches on asphalt roads. But these are always quiet country roads, generally free of traffic.

If you are walking on a Sunday or a *fiesta,* choose as remote a location as you can find. That is the day when Spaniards pack up their cars and head for the wide open spaces — to hunt, to gather wild mushrooms, to collect water from mountain *fonts*, to picnic or simply to enjoy a drive. Roads will be busy, and picnic sites with benches and car access could well be chock-a-block.

Unless you are doing one of the walks close to the tourist beat, the accepted greeting for other walkers or for farmers is the Valencian *Bon día*, rather than the Spanish *Buenos días*. It will always elicit a hearty response.

Please read and *heed* the country code on page 11.

Grading, waymarking, maps, GPS

We've tried to give you a quick overview of each walk's **grade** in the Contents. But all of our walks have shorter or alternative versions, and in the Contents we've only had space to show the *lowest* grade of a *main* walk: for full details, including both easier and tougher versions, see the walk itself. Here is a brief overview of the four grades:

- ● very easy — more or less level (perhaps with a short climb to a viewpoint); good surfaces underfoot; easily followed
- ● easy-moderate — ascents/descents of no more than about 300-500m/1000-1800ft; good surfaces underfoot; easily followed
- ● moderate-strenuous — ascents/descents may be over 500m/1800ft; variable surfaces underfoot; possible route-finding problems
- ● only suitable for very sure-footed, experienced hillwalkers; may be very long; possible route-finding problems

Any of the above grades may be followed by:

- ⦙ *possibility* of vertigo — for those with no head for heights at all
- ⦙⦙ *danger* of vertigo — you must have a very good head for heights

Assigning grades to walks is *very* subjective. When grading our walks, we have tried to describe the effort required, the state of the paths, and the ease of navigation. You need not be an expert or even a habitual walker to tackle most of our walks, but a reasonable level of fitness and stamina, as well as some mountain 'sense', is assumed. *Be sure to read through the whole description of a walk before setting out,* so that you know *exactly* what to expect and what to take with you. *If the main walk looks too strenuous,* see if there are any short or alternative versions which are less demanding. You need look no further than the picnic suggestions on pages 10-15 to find a wide selection of *very easy walks.*

Our **frequent time checks** are *not* meant to be followed minute-by-minute throughout the walk, but to indicate the easily-monitored *time difference* between various points. Check our notes frequently, to avoid missing turn-offs or landmarks. Our **overall timings** *do not include any stops.* Allow time for lunch, photography, bird-watching and botanising. Take account of the weather, too. Hot sun, driving rain and strong winds will affect your progress. *Do* compare your pace with ours on one or two short walks *before* setting out on a long hike and adjust as necessary.

Most of the paths are now **waymarked**; you will be following many yellow/white waymarked PR ('Pequeño Recorrido') short-distance walks. You will also see the red/white striped waymarks of the GR7 ('Gran Recorrido') long-distance footpath. Other paths may have been marked by local walking groups — perhaps with coloured dots, arrows or cairns — or a combination of all of these. Our walks usually coincide with waymarked routes but seldom follow them all the way — *so don't get carried away by the markings; read our instructions.*

Our **maps**, based on Spanish military surveys, have been thoroughly updated for this edition. Together with our walking notes, they should suffice for all the walks in this book. Or you can order 1:50,000 or 1:25,000 government or commercial maps from your usual map supplier.

Free **GPS track** downloads are available for all our walks: see the Costa Blanca page on the Sunflower website. Please bear in mind, however, that GPS readings should *never* be relied upon as your sole reference point, as conditions can change overnight. *But even if you don't use GPS,* it's great fun opening our GPX files in Google Earth to preview the walks in advance!

Where to stay

If you take a package holiday you will undoubtedly find yourself in one of the **coastal towns**. If travelling independently and keen to walk, you might prefer to stay **in the mountains**, where there are a few *pensiones* and *hostales* (some English-run). Even in the smallest villages there may be someone willing to offer you basic hospitality. Tourist offices provide a list of accommodation, but it is by no means complete — village bars and the web are better sources of ideas.

There are plenty of **campsites**; we have visited Vall d'Alcalà (good facilities, uninspiring site), Vall d'Ebo (basic but grassy, with plenty of trees), Font Mariola (huge commercial site, with all facilities, and, less than 1km away, a much more attractive, free municipal site, with a *font*), and Font Roja (reasonable facilities and no charge). On the coast, a site we have *not* visited is near Campello harbour (www.campingcostablanca.com).

Weather

With care, you can walk comfortably in this region all year round — as long as you **heed the weather signs and carry appropriate equipment**. The best time to walk is undoubtedly spring, when the hillsides are carpeted with a huge variety of colourful and delicate flowers and herbs — providing a feast for butterflies and birds and a great spectacle for walkers. But the limestone rock and the nature of the climate ensures that you will find some flowers in bloom in the mountains at any time of year.

There can be **frost** in the mountains in winter with **snow** on the highest peaks and **strong winds** in exposed areas may make it feel very cold sometimes. February and November can be quite wet; **heavy storms**, which cause damage to tracks and paths, often occur in September and early October. Such storms, though not usually very long-lasting, can be quite unexpected and frighteningly fierce, so make sure you are prepared. The strength of the **sun** should not be ignored at any time of the year, and it can be blisteringly hot from May to October.

What to take

The mountains of the Costa Blanca are unlikely to present the sort of extreme weather conditions that might be encountered at home but, nevertheless, you should equip yourself for all eventualities. The sun can be strong at any time of the year, so **suncream, sunhat and long-sleeved shirt** should always be taken with you on walks. According to the season and prevailing weather conditions, you must judge what **extra items of clothing** you might need. Storms *can* occur in summer, and even on a bright sunny day it can be very chilly at high altitude — so take **warm and waterproof clothing** on mountain walks. The whole area tends to be very rocky underfoot and **stout, thick-soled shoes, preferably with ankle support, are a must for all but one or two of the walks.** Unless you are walking in extremely bad weather you should not require heavy boots, but for comfort we certainly recommend lightweight hiking boots or shoes. Paths and tracks can be very muddy for a day or so after heavy rain, with the clay-like soil clinging to your boots. The other essential is **water**. Bottled water is widely available. There are *fonts* on a few of the walks but in summer months you are quite likely to find they are dry. For all longer walks you should take a **picnic lunch**.

For each walk, we specify any additional items you will require. We have sometimes included **compass** directions as extra confirmation of the route to take — if you are a compass user like us. But Sunflower have also made **free GPS tracks** available for all the walks; these can be downloaded from the Costa Blanca page on the Sunflower website.

For **emergencies** it is always wise to carry a **first-aid kit,** high energy food, extra water, a couple of large black plastic bags, whistle, torch, warm clothing and a **mobile/smartphone** (the emergency number throughout Europe is 112).

Walk 1: Views over Denia from the Camí de la Colonia. Although this is easy walking (and popular with cyclists), most of the paths on Montgó are rocky and, while wide enough to be comfortable, they demand care.

Nuisances

Dogs might be encountered as you pass close to farms, but they are usually chained up or fenced in and when they're loose they seldom present a threat. However, the sudden noise of their barking as they sense an alien presence can give you a fright and if they do bound out of a gateway straight towards you, you should slow down but continue on your way without showing panic or aggression. If dogs worry you, invest in a 'Dog Dazer', an ultrasonic dog deterrent. These are widely available on the web.

It is unlikely that you will have a problem with either **snakes** or **scorpions**, but you should be aware of the possibility. In warm weather we see snakes quite regularly, usually slithering out of our way at the side of a path. The only poisonous snake is a viper with a triangular yellowish head and a zigzag line down its spine. A bite from one of these needs urgent medical attention. Scorpion stings should also be treated quickly. But you will avoid problems if you are careful: keep to the path, do not disturb rocks or stones, and think twice before sitting on a drystone wall.

The main **hunting season** is from mid-October to February, when hunters and their dogs will be about on Thursdays and at weekends (especially on Sundays).

Organisation of the walks

The area covered by this guide is bounded by the coast in the east, the Serra de Benicadell in the north, the serras of Mariola and Maigmó in the west, and the city of Alicante in the south. This inverted triangle includes a very complex topography, with over 35 named serras, both rugged and gentle, interspersed by a large number of picturesque valleys.

We have chosen to split the walks into six groups, categorised by the coastal strip in the east, the serras forming the western border of the area, and those based around groups of valleys going roughly west to east:

Walks 1-5: coastal strip from Dénia to Benidorm
Walks 6-9: Serpis and Gallinera valleys
Walks 10-12: Laguar and Jalón valleys
Walks 13-16: Guadalest, Algar and Sella valleys
Walks 17-22: Alcoi area
Walks 23-26: serras of Carrasqueta and Maigmó

You will probably start with walks closest to your base, but all are quite accessible from any of the coastal resorts. You'll find an overview of the walk areas on the touring map, and a quick flip through the book reveals at least one photo for each walk.

Finally, we would like to **highlight five walks** which will give you a good cross-section of the terrain and landscape. **Walk 1** takes you to a mountain summit; **Walk 6** leads along a beautiful river valley and up to a castle; **Walk 10** traverses amazing Mozarabic trails from the Middle Ages; **Walk 13** follows some gentle mountain valleys under the highest mountain in Alicante province; and **Walk 19** visits 17th-century 'snow wells' (*cavas*) on a high mountain ridge.

Each walk begins with planning information: times/distances, grade, equipment and transport. For some of the main walks we suggest possible alternatives and give a short version where feasible. Before the detailed description of the route there is a general introduction to give you a 'feel' for the landscape.

Below is a key to the **symbols** on the walking maps:

motorway	spring *(font)*, well, etc	church, chapel.shrine
dual carriageway	*P* picnic suggestion (see pages 10-15)	charcoal burners' terrace, limekiln
main road	best views	watchtower
secondary road	bus stop	cemetery
narrow road	railway station	picnic tables
unmade road, street	car parking	transmitter.pylon
jeep track, etc	building.enclosure	rock formation
path, steps	castle or fort.ruined	mill
main walk	quarry, mine. cave	electricity sub-station
alternative walk	waypoint	snow well

See also Dénia plan on page 9 and photos on pages 11 and 42-43
Distance: 13km/8mi; 5h48min
Grade: ● ? quite strenuous, with a climb and descent of 640m/2100ft on good, but rocky paths. You must be surefooted and have a head for heights. Well waymarked and signposted. Avoid windy days.
Equipment: see page 42; also walking boots with ankle support, compass/GPS, plenty of water
How to get there and return: 🚗 to/from Montgó Natural Park (38° 49.106'N, 0° 6.399'E; see Car tour 1 just after the 93km-point). Or on foot from the Alqueries railway station: walk up Camí del Pou de la Montanya, just next to the station; it's signposted to the park and the Ermita Pare Pere (add about 20min walk each way; see plan on page 9).

Short walk: Cova de l'Aigua.
4.7km/3mi; 1h30min. ● Moderate, with an ascent/descent of 300m/1000ft. Equipment as page 42. Access/return as main walk. Follow the main walk to the 19min-point (❷) and turn left. A few minutes later take the marked path on the right to the **Cova de l'Aigua** (**a**). Return the same way.

Alternative walk: Cova de l'Aigua and Cova del Camell. 12.5km/7.8mi; 4h. ● Grade, equipment and transport as Short walk. Follow the Short walk to the **Cova de l'Aigua** (**a**), but turn right when you come back down to the Camí de la Colònia (43min). Continue as far as the **Cova del Camell** (❼; 2h15min) and return the same way.

The Parc Natural del Montgó takes its name from the forbidding-looking mountain shown on page 11, which forms the backdrop to the resorts of Dénia and Xàbia. This walk ascends its northeast face, descends south towards Xàbia, then skirts the foot of the mountain on an old trail.

Start out at the DENIA ENTRANCE to the **Parc Natural** (❶): take the surfaced track behind the chain barrier, by an INFORMATION BOARD for the routes in the natural park. The trail (marked orange and yellow) zigzags up the lower slopes to the old track, the **Camí de la Colònia** (❷; **19min**), which contours round the foot of Montgó. Turn right (you will return from the left, and *the Short and Alternative walks turn left now*). The humidity on this face of the mountain encourages the growth of lush ferns, but has not prevented fires. When the *camí* peters out, turn sharp left on a path (SIGNPOST; **31min**) which begins to climb quite steeply as it approaches a sheer cliff.

A short level stretch under the cliff offers a brief respite (**56min**), just before you meet another narrow signposted path coming up from the Cova de l'Aigua. Fork right here (❸; **1h03min**) and head uphill again on a steep, rocky path lined with wild flowers. Just before a crest (**1h28min**), a path near Penya de l'Aguila comes in from the right by a GREEN-SIGNPOSTED route to Jesús Pobre (❹). If you are very lucky here, you may see eagles (*águilas*) after which the Penya is named.

From the crest head left on an obvious path lined with

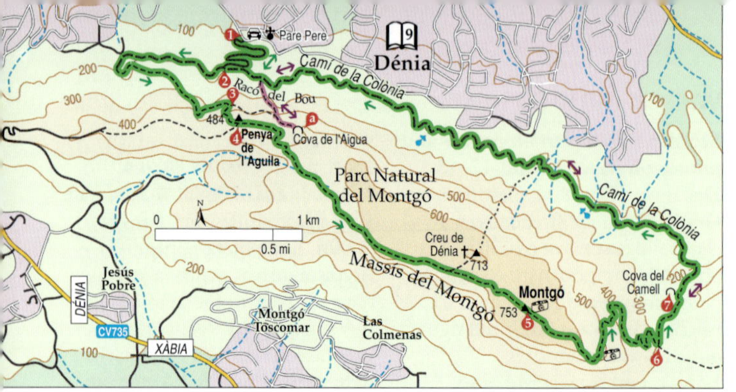

lavender and rosemary. Eventually (**2h05min**) a clear path marked with stones leads left to a large cross (**Creu de Dénia**) on a peak, but keep straight ahead with the ORANGE AND GREEN WAYMARKS. Your path, sometimes narrow and exposed, snakes along to a lone pine and a cave, and then up to the TOP OF **Montgó** (**5**; 753m/2470ft; **2h45min**). Inland the serras unfold layer by layer; along the coast, you can see as far as Gandía to the north and Calp to the south. On a clear day Ibiza is visible on the eastern horizon.

Looking inland, your descent path lies over to the left, within five metres of the summit, heading a little east of south. Clear WAYMARKS guide you: the first section is a bit of a scramble down the rocky slope. The scramble ends (**3h12min**) and you join the well-built path shown on pages 42-43, which zigzags all the way down the middle slopes. As you get lower, look down and locate your goal: a clear track originating in a *barranc* and winding round the foot of the mountain to the left.

Just after a short uphill section, Xàbia comes into view ahead. Ignore all the steep short-cut paths through the thickening vegetation, so as not to miss the SIGNPOSTED FORK (**6**; **4h**) which indicate your route to Dénia. The route leads you over the rocks and along the right bank of a *barranc*, to a path from where the holding wall of the track you saw from above is visible. Descend into the *barranc*, passing the **Cova del Camell** (**7**; **4h13min**).

Cross the *barranc* and climb to the track above, the **Camí de la Colònia**. Flat and partly cobbled, it provides ever-changing views over the coast. After passing an old KILN and a CISTERN, you will meet another, dauntingly steep, unofficial route up to the summit. Beyond two more CISTERNS and a RUINED HOUSE, you pass the steep signposted PATH TO THE COVA DE L'AIGUA (**5h25min**), an impressive natural cavity with a permanent spring, which in the past provided much of Dénia's water. (Allow an extra 20min return for this detour.) Continue on the *camí* to the junction with your outward track (**2**; **5h30min**). Turn right downhill, back to the PARK ENTRANCE (**1**; **5h48min**).

Equipment for all walks: see page 42; also swimming gear for Walks 2c-d. Trainers should suffice as footwear.

Distance, grade, access: see individual walks.

a **Cap de Sant Antoni.** 4.8km/3mi; 1h40min. ● Easy, with an ascent/descent of 160m/525ft. Access by 🚗 or on foot to the port at the northern end of Xàbia. See text below.

b **Els Molins.** 5km/3mi; 1h23min (with detour 7km/4.3mi; 2h20min). The main walk is an ● easy stroll; the optional detour is very steep and ● strenuous and requires great care. 🚗 to the *zona recreativa* on the Cap de Sant Antoni road (38° 48.368'N,

0° 11.154'E; see Car tour 1 from about 76km). Ample parking and ⊼, water taps; pleasantly set amidst pines. See text page 48.

c **Cap Prim.** 2.2km/1.3mi; 35min. ● Easy. 🚗 to the Creu del Portitxol, a stone cross on the CV742 (38° 45.387'N, 0° 13.138'E; the 55km-point on Car tour 1). Pick up text on page 49. **Photo on page 11.**

d **Calp cliffs and calas.** 6km/3.8mi; 1h50min. ● Easy. 🚐 bus or 🚗 car to Cala Calaga (from the 39km-point of Car tour 1; 38° 39.087'N, 0° 4.641'E), or walk to Cala Calalga at the eastern end of Calp's promenade, just beyond the Hotel Esmeralda.

These four short walks provide a good cross-section of coastal scenery in this delightful area. The secluded coves, rugged headlands and old windmills capture the beauty of the landscape around Xàbia and Calp.

Start Walk a at the PORT in **Xàbia** (**①**): follow the coast road past the RED CROSS BUILDING. Just beyond the CLUB NAÚTICO, when the road ends (**6min**), go up some concrete steps to the left. These give way to a narrow rocky PATH, the yellow/white-waymarked PR-CV 355, which snakes up the hillside. At a fork, go left, along the left-hand side of a *barranc*. Cross this stream bed (**19min**) and turn right along its far bank, heading east towards Cap de Sant Antoni. At **25min** ignore a path downhill to the right and continue gently climbing. In spring the scent of rosemary and pine mingle tantalisingly, and in autumn the slopes are clad with heather. The clear path contours round the slopes and circles the head of another *barranc* (**34min**). Some 350m/yds further on, ignore a path up to the left. After another 250m the path forks again (**46min**). The right fork goes to the lighthouse on the headland at Cap de Sant Antoni. Take the left fork, which leads you up to a CAR PARK and *mirador* with a water tap on the main Cap de Sant Antoni road (**②**; **49min**). From here you have a fantastic view down to Xàbia. Cap de Sant Antoni is 300m away to the right (**ⓐ**). To the left, eight minutes' walk away, is a *zona recreativa* (**③**) where you could link up with Walk 2b. Otherwise, walk back to the PORT (**①**; **1h40min**).

Start Walk b at the *zona recreativa* on the CAP DE SANT ANTONI ROAD (**③**): take the wide gravel track signedposted

'MOLINS' which heads off to the left (part of the CV-PR 355). Follow it for about 1.5km, to a T-junction with an old abandoned *cuartel* (military barracks; **❹**; **20min**) just off to the left. Turn left*. You pass the *cuartel* and some villas, and reach the MAIN CAP DE SANT ANTONI ROAD (**25min**). Cross the road and walk up CAMÍ DEL MONASTIR, which follows the boundary walls of the imposing **Santuari Mare de Déu** (**❺**). This narrow cypress-lined lane is asphalted at first but soon becomes unsurfaced. As it sweeps left (you will return this way later) go straight ahead (**31min**) and you will see the FIRST WINDMILL *(molin)* at the top of the **Plana dels Molins** crest.

There are 12 mills in all, 11 of them lined up along this crest. Take the path going up to the first mill on the right and continue along past the others, some of which are now privately owned and which you skirt round on a path on the Xàbia side of the cliff. A narrow asphalt road (**41min**) takes you the remaining 100 metres to the path up left to the LAST THREE in this line of mills (**❻**; **46min**), from where the views are spectacular (*P*2b) and someone has thoughtfully placed a picnic table. The mills, built between the 14th and 19th centuries, were positioned to catch the best of the winds, vital for the grinding of the grain once grown on the terraces. It is over a hundred years since they

---

*If you are surefooted and agile, you can take a 1h detour: turn *right* here. After five minutes (250m), on a left-hand bend just after a wall, take a path off right, past a *font* and a little water tank. This old smugglers' route crosses an open area then descends very steeply between two *barrancs*. The path is cairned as it veers left into the most westerly *barranc*, where you pass first the **Cova Negra** and then come to the spectacular **Cova Foradada** (**❺**), almost at sea level — once inhabited seasonally by Late Stone Age nomads. Retrace your steps to the junction.

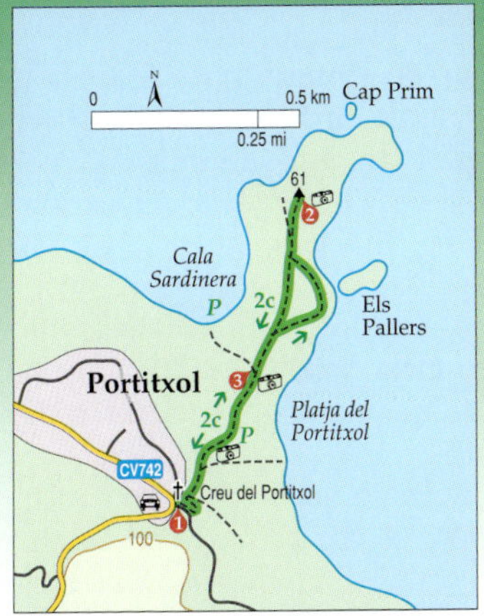

were last in use, but only one of them is a complete ruin. The towers of the rest remain solid although they have all lost their cones and sails.

Leaving the PR 355, retrace your steps to the point where you reached the crest (**55min**). The path which runs downward below the mills winds its way into Xàbia, but you turn left, back towards the *santuario*. After about 60m/yds turn right on the unsurfaced road. This leads past a STONE CROSS and the 12TH MILL (**7**). Notice the game bird breeding aviary nearby on the left — sadly no longer used — and turn left on the asphalted CALLE CUESTA DE SAN ANTONIO (a right turn here leads down into Xàbia port). Cross the MAIN CAP DE SANT ANTONI ROAD (**1h08min**), go straight ahead and, after 100m/yds, turn right on a narrow track. This joins your outward track (**1h11min**). Turn right, back to the *zona recreativa* (**3**; **1h23min**).

Start Walk c at the **Creu del Portitxol** (**1**): looking out from the cross, you will see the island of Portitxol to the right and the rocky headland of Cap Prim to the left. Directly below, the GREEN/WHITE WAYMARKED SL-CV 98 path winds downhill and then runs alongside some old grassy terraces, beyond which there are pines (**P2c**). Take this path which leads down from the cross, past an INFORMATION BOARD, but turn sharp left at a junction after only about 50m/yds. Descend through the wooded terraces, passing occasional waymarks. The path takes you to the edge of the cliff, then bears left along the eastern side of the headland. At **9min** the view of Montgó looming ahead is probably the finest you will ever have of that forbidding mountain (shown on page 11). Ignore the first couple of eroded paths left to Cala Sardinera — *don't* be tempted to make your way down any of these shortcuts. Wait till you reach the way-marked junction to the *cala* on your return. For now, continue to the highest point on **Cap Prim** (**❷**; **19min**). If it's not windy, and you feel brave, you can go a little further out on the sheer rocky promontory, but we suggest you just admire the views, before retracing your steps for about 200m/yds to a junction. Take the right fork now, along the western side of the promontory, passing above Cala Sardinera. Just a little over 100m/yds after rejoining your outward path, you pass the WAYMARKED PATH (**❸**) down to **Cala Sardinera** (*P*2c) again, should you want to visit it. Or continue straight back up to the **Creu del Portitxol** (**❶**; **35min**).

   Walk d is an out and back walk, so go as far as you wish. **Start out** at **Cala Calalga** (**❶**), at the eastern end of the promenade in **Calp**. Continue northeast, up the road, and turn right on a PR-signposted path to 'PTO BASSETES'(**4min**). What was once an eroded narrow cliff path, with sheer drops to the sea, has been transformed by the construction of flights of steps (some steep), gravelled paths, paved walkways and log fencing. So this walk is now accessible to far more people, who can enjoy the stunning views of the Penyal d'Ifach and Cap de Moraira, as well as opportunities to explore tiny *calas* — coves. You pass **Cala el Mallorqui** (**13min**), followed by an interestingly-painted villa and then reach the marina at **Ses Bassetes** (**23min**). Now go up the steep hill and follow the path alongside the road as far as the **Mirador ses Bassetes** at the KM2 marker (**❷**; **32min**). From the *mirador* the walkway continues to **Cala Fustera** (**❸**; **41min**) and **Cala Pinet**. A little further on there is another delightful cove (**54min**; *P*2d). It's secluded, has flat rocks to sit on and rock pools — altogether an excellent spot to linger before returning the same way to **Calp** (**1h50min**).

Els Molins at Xàbia
(Picnic 2b, Walk 2b)

Walk 3: VUELTA DE OLTA (OLTA CIRCUIT)

See also photo on page 19
Distance: 11km/6.8mi; 3h20min
Grade: ● ‡ moderate, with climbs and corresponding descents of about 360m/1180ft overall. Mostly on easy tracks, but surefootedness is essential on a few short sections. The initial climb to the circuit track is steep. Navigation is straightforward; the circuit track and alternative paths have good yellow/white PR waymarks and signposts (PR-CV 340).
Equipment: see page 42
How to get there and return: 🚂, 🚐 or 🚗 to Calp station (38° 38.984'N, 0° 1.992'E). Motorists can reduce walking time by about 15min and 100m/330ft: From Calp station, cross the railway lines, then follow the signs for 'Monte Olta, Zona de Acampada' (3km), where there is a tiny car park (**a**; 38° 39.507'N, 0° 1.590'E). From the campsite a narrow path (PR-CV 340) leads up to a track. Turn left, then 3min later, turn left again at the circuit track. Follow the main walk from the 2h10min-point to the 2h30min-point, then continue on the circuit track by picking up the main walk at the 33min-point.

Alternative walk: Oltá summits.
Allow a *minimum* of 4km/2.5mi; 2h *from the Ermita Vella*. ● ‡ Moderate, with ascents/descents of at least 250m/820ft. Equipment as page 42 plus walking boots; access as main walk. See the map: various paths explore the mountain summits. You could, for instance, follow the main walk past the 33min-point (**2**) and after the sweeping right-hand bend fork *right*. In ten minutes a sign for the Oltá summit signals a scramble up a rocky gully. The gradient eventually eases and in about 20min you reach a junction on the plateau (**9**), where a path goes left to the southern summit and straight on leads to the northern summit via the ruins of Corralet. Allow about 15min to the southern summit and 30-35 to the northern — *each way*. Or follow the main walk to (**3**), from where a path rises directly to the Corralet ruins.

T his clockwise walk around the Oltá peaks undulates roughly between the 300m and 400m contours. Each time you emerge from the shade of fragrant pine trees you will have spectacular views over Calp and the coastline or towards the serrated ridges of surrounding serras.

Start out at **Calp** STATION (**1**): cross the RAILWAY LINES just beyond the station, walk up the road a short distance and take a road *left* with a small PR sign to Oltá. (Motorists go *right* here for 'MONTE OLTÁ, ZONA DE ACAMPADA'.) After about 50m/yds, fork right, heading towards Oltá. Pass POSTBOXES on your left and continue about 350m/yds to the top of the hill, then fork right again. When the road ends, take a forestry track at the left of a house (**8min**). At **15min** fork right again and, just after, ignore a track coming in from the right. Ignore a track coming in from the left and another joining from the right (**20min**). At a three-way junction, where there are fine views ahead to the Serra de Toix (**24min**), go straight on. Ignore a track to the left (**31min**) and reach the CIRCUIT TRACK (**2**; **33min**), with an INFORMATION BOARD, and the **Ermita Vella** behind (*P3*).

Turn left; the crags of Oltá's southern summit now rise steeply above you, as you rise gradually for 100m/yds. After a sweeping right-hand bend, take the next track left ('OLTA SUR'). *(But for the Alternative walk, fork right.)* You are now on level ground again, and Calp is spread out before you, from its southern harbour under the Morro de Toix to the Penyal d'Ifach guarding its northern harbour.

Reach a large open area on the left (**40min**) and two minutes later, ignore a track going left. As you continue, the panorama now includes the Mascarat Gorge with its three tunnels overlooked by the ruins of Calp Castle. Beyond the castle, the Serra Gelada shelters Benidorm from the sea. The track undulates as it contours around the southwestern flank of Oltá.

Throughout the traverse of this western flank the peaks of the Serra Bernia dominate the skyline to the west, more of it coming into view with every step you take. Watch as the whole length of this magnificent ridge, shown opposite, opens out before you. Pass a sign, 'CIM D'OLTÁ' at the **Barranc de la Mola** (❸; another access to the Alternative walk) and 350m/yds further on, a RUINED HOUSE perched on the hillside (**1h**), beyond which you ignore a track coming in from the left. Ignore another track coming in from the left very shortly. At this point take note of the 'needles' below Oltá's north summit and another abandoned house. At a T-junction (❹; **1h14min**) turn sharp right to reach this house, the **Finca Pastor** (❺; **1h23min**), from where the photo opposite was taken.

Now, as you climb steeply, Oltá's northern summit (591m/

Bernia Ridge, from the Finca Pastor

1940ft) towers above you. Pass below the 'needles' and an interesting rock formation called '**Olta's Finger**' (**6**), ignoring firebreak tracks off to the right. The track descends to meet another track at a T-junction (**1h34min**). Turn right uphill here for 'LA CANAL' and head for yet another RUIN situated between the north summit and Little Oltá (424m/1390ft). The front of the house, on the pass of **La Canal** (**7**), is a good place to take a break.

As you continue, the track narrows to a path and begins descending, first gradually, then ever more steeply. Watch for the waymarks on this skiddy descent. The surrounding area is covered in low scrub and there may be fallen trees. Join a forestry track (**1h52min**) and turn right. Now ignore all forks until the track curves left and you reach a sign for the PR-CV 340 and the 'ZONA ACAMPADA', where you turn right. Then wind through pines, often alive with the twittering of coal tits and long tailed tits. You enjoy glimpses of the coast, from the Cap de Moraira to Calp, with the Penyal d'Ifach and Calp's salt pans dominating the scene (photo on page 19).

At a junction (**8**; **2h10min**), turn right on a forestry road. *(Motorists using the alternative starting point at the campsite come in from the left and go back the same way at this junction.)* Ignore tracks off to houses or beckoning you up the mountain. Soon the southern summit of Oltá (539m/ 1968ft) appears ahead of you. At the junction (**2h30min**) your circuit is complete: turn left, retracing your outward route back to **Calp** STATION (**1**; **3h20min**).

See photo on page 134
Distance: 12km/7.5mi; 3h39min
Grade: ● strenuous, with an ascent/descent of 570m/1870ft; well waymarked PR-CV 289 throughout (yellow/white flashes)
Equipment: see page 42
How to get there and return: 🚗 car to the 6km-point in Car tour 4: instead of turning left to Sella, turn right into Finestrat. At the main crossroads in the town centre, turn left for 'Font del Molí' and drive 1km to the *font*. Park just beyond the *font* on the right (38° 34.702'N, 0° 12.503'W). 🚌 to the crossroads in the centre of Finestrat. Walk up the hill to Font del Molí (25 min). Return bus times are variable — ask your driver. If necessary get a taxi or walk back and catch a bus at Carrefour/La Marina.

Short walk: Font del Molí — Campana's lower slopes. 6km/ 3.8mi; 1h43min. ● Easy, with one short ascent/descent of 150m/500ft. Start as for the main walk and turn right on the track at the 1min-point. Follow the yellow and white PR waymarks (this is the end of main walk, but in reverse). Meet a track at a signpost and turn right (**5**; 35min) but, after just 150m/yds (on the first bend), turn left on a track and immediately left again on a cairned path. Descend gradually through old terraces and pine woods, cross a *barranc* and meet a wider path waymarked in red (**6**; 53min). Turn sharp right. Cross the *barranc* again and then go straight across a track (1h08min). When you meet a track by a ruined house (**7**; 1h19min), turn right, then turn right again on a road. Within 150m/yds pass a road on the left (**8** — a direct route back to Finestrat, 25 minutes from here; it briefly becomes a path as it passes a *font*). To return to Font del Molí, take the road going left only 10m further on; it snakes round the hillside above a reservoir, back to Font del Molí (**1**; 1h43min).

Each of the four faces of Campana has its own mood and its own distinctive vegetation. With views changing spectacularly as you move around the mountain on this classic route, you will find this a most satisfying walk.

Start out at **Font del Molí** (**1**): continue up the road following fingerposts for the PR-CV 289. You pass a track to the right (**1min**); this is your return route (*and the Short walk turns right here*). Just after crossing a bridge over a WATER CHANNEL (**11min**), take the wide track uphill to the right. After 30m you come to a signpost for the PR-CV 289 and turn left for the 'COLL DEL POUET', ignoring the trail ('KM VERTICAL') signed straight on to the summit of Campana. Soon you enjoy views to Aitana, Penya Sella and the 'sharks' teeth' of Castellets to the left and the west face of Campana rising steeply to the right. You climb through slopes covered in rosemary and bell heather, with spectacular views (**50min**).

Still climbing quite steadily, you'll soon round the bend to the north side of the mountain, where the cooler slopes are coloured with the blue, purple and yellow of rosemary, heather and gorse. Rounding another bend (**1h09min**), notice a *finca*

(Mas de l'Oficial) below and the cliffs of Ponoch ahead to the left. Climb to the right of a MOUNTAINEERS' HUT (**2**; **Refugi Vera Catral**; **1h34min**); the path broadens as it rises to the signposted **Coll del Pouet** (**3**; **1h46min**), an open grassy area with a large flat rock — a good spot for a rest.

Five paths meet at this pass. Your incoming path continues slightly downhill. Another path comes up from the Mas de l'Oficial. A PR-marked path (PR-CV 13) goes left towards the cliffs below Ponoch, eventually leading to Polop. And finally, to the right, your onward track goes uphill (PR-CV 289 'FOIA CAC, FONT SOLSIDA'). Follow it up and, as it turns right, continue the circuit by going left (**1h50min**), now contouring round towards the eastern face of Campana. As the Serra Gelada comes into view, the path drops to run below a sheer cliff, passing the **Font de la Solsida** (**4**; now dry). Then the path continues under the softer eastern face of Campana. At first you pass through low scrub but later through rock and scree, contouring at around 900m and ignoring all paths up the mountain.

The south face comes into view (**2h24min**) as you head around a *barranc* descending from the summit. Cross a flat open area and soon begin a steady descent, heading towards the western end of the Cortina Ridge. Roldan's Notch (also called 'El Portell') is clearly visible on your right as the path steepens and zigzags to ease the descent over the rocks. When you reach an obvious junction of paths on a level stretch in amongst pine trees (**2h49min**), fork right. This quite wide path crosses a *barranc*, runs through a pine wood and eventually passes old TERRACES (**3h01min**).

You cross a track at a signpost (**5**; **3h04min**; *the Short walk turns right here*) and soon begin a longish descent on a sometimes stony or rocky path. The path meets a lane/track which you follow to a T-junction (**3h31min**): go left, cross the deep WATER CHANNEL and, a couple of minutes later go left down the road, back to **Font del Moli** (**1**; **3h39min**).

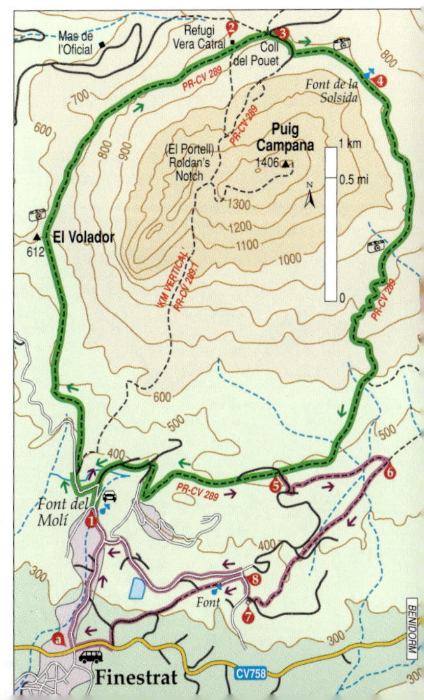

Walk 5: SERRA GELADA — FROM BENIDORM TO ALBIR

See also town plan page 8
Distance: 10km/6.2mi; 4h
Grade: ● ‼ strenuous, with steep ascents and corresponding descents of 625m/2050ft overall. You must be surefooted and have a head for heights. Paths are often eroded and sometimes uncomfortably close to the edge of the sheer cliffs (**danger of vertigo**). Navigation is fairly straightforward, with yellow/white waymarking (some of it faded) and cairns past Alt de la Montera.
Equipment: see page 42; also proper walking boots or shoes, compass/gps, plenty of water
How to get there: 🚗 taxi or on foot to Avenida Alcalde Manuel Catalán Chana at the eastern end of Platja de Llevant — on the bend just as the road rounds the headland at Punta del Pinet; no suitable car parking
To return: 🚌 from Albir; alight at Ametlla de Mar if you parked your car at the eastern end of Platja de Llevant (38° 31.942'N, 0° 6.409'W) or get off in the centre of Benidorm.

Short walks (access as main walk; equipment as page 42)
1 Benidorm — Alt de la Montera — Benidorm. 4km/2.5mi; 1h50min. ● Fairly strenuous climb/descent of 330m/1080ft, but no danger of vertigo. Follow the main walk for 56min (**❸**), then return the same way.
2 Benidorm — La Torre — Benidorm. 3km/1.9mi; 1h15min. ● Easy. Go through the gap in the wooden railings at Punta del Pinet and head down to the cove below (Cala Almadraba). Take the path round to the headland above the next cove, Cala Tio Ximo. From the roundabout here follow an asphalt road to the next headland, then continue on a footpath **Punta de la Escaleta** (*P*5). Now climb a path up to another asphalt road and follow it to the ruins of **La Torre** (**❽**; 35min), a 17th-century watchtower with a superb outlook to the cliffs of the Serra Gelada. To return to (**❶**), retrace steps or follow the road.

Despite its proximity to Benidorm, the Serra Gelada is no mean mountain and must be treated with respect. From the landward side its undulating silhouette appears benign, but from the sea its sheer, stepped cliffs present a formidable picture. This exhilarating hike follows the cliff edge, with fantastic views.

View from the Camí Vell del Far back up to the relay station at Alt del Governador. Major gullies are crossed before reaching this highest point in the range (438m/1440ft).

Start out at Punta del Pinet (**1**), walking away from Benidorm. When the wooden railings end, continue sharply left up Calle Sierra Dorada. At the T-junction turn right ('Todas Direcciones'; **8min**) and at the roundabout take the road to the right signed to 'La Cruz'. The tedious climb is over when the road ends abruptly below our first goal, the **Mirador de la Cruz** (**2**; **30min**). Before the road ends, rise up to the cross on an obvious path — for good views over the antennas of Radio Benidorm and the tower on Punta de la Escaleta (Short walk 2).

From here the walk will progress along the ridge, heading generally northeast, alternately climbing to the cliff tops and then dropping steeply to cross the gullies. Either take the narrow path going down to the right just past the cross, or continue on the main path; the two paths rejoin a few metres below. Descend to a fork and bear left above a *barranc* on a well-trodden rocky path. It takes you round the head of the *barranc* (**38min**) and starts climbing to the top of the first cliff. This spot, popular with retired expatriates and locals alike, is marked with a large cairn (**Alt de la Montera**; **3**; 338m/1100ft; **56min**). It's the serra's southern peak. *Short walk 1 turns back here.*

From here the walk, sporadically way-marked with yellow/white flashes, makes for the end of the serra, where the antenna of the relay station is visible. But there are a lot of ups and downs to negotiate before you reach it. From the myriad of small paths round the cairn, take the most obvious one along the cliff top (*the only waymarked route*). When you come to the end of the level section, take the rough, rocky waymarked path; it descends into a gully, close to the edge of the cliff. Cross

the gully (**1h08min**) and, having lost about 50m/165ft of altitude, you must now regain it. Continue within a few metres/yards of the cliff edge to the next peak. Cairns supplement the waymarks as you head down into the next, shallower gully. As you cross it (**1h25min**), you can see two routes up to the next peak. Make your choice of path and reach the top at **1h31min**. Below and ahead of you is the little island, Penyes de Arabí, dwarfed by the towering cliffs of the Serra Gelada.

The path, clear but steep, and only about 10m/yds from the cliff edge, zigzags down into the next gully, before rising past the ruins of what was probably an ANIMAL PEN (**2h**). After crossing the small hump by the ruins, it descends to cross another gully. From here a steep climb (sometimes on all fours!) brings you to the penultimate peak (**2h30min**), from where you can see the asphalt road to the relay station. Now the path descends into the last gully, moves away from the cliffs, and JOINS THE ROAD (**4**; **2h40min**). Turn right and follow the road steeply uphill.

The surrounds of the RELAY STATION AT THE SUMMIT of **Alt del Governador** (**5**; **3h**) are closed, and you descend about 50m/yds below its gates. Watch for your descent path, on the left, signalled by a signpost: 'FAR DE L'ALBIR'. It is fairly clear and, once on it, you will see WAYMARKING, sometimes supplemented by ARROWS. The resort and beach at Albir lie far below, and the path heads in that general direction, initially contouring below the relay station. It passes under electricity cables and begins to descend steeply. Ignore short-cuts as it zigzags down, following the line of the cables. When the path forks (**3h10min**), go right through a pine wood. After an open, fairly level section, the path splits again (**3h20min**): take either fork — they meet up again about five minutes later.

Eventually you wind down to a FIVE-WAY JUNCTION (**3h35min**), at a flattish piece of ground level with apartments on the left. Go right and keep following the cables, ignoring all crossing paths. You can see the road to the Albir lighthouse passing through a tunnel below. When you reach this road (CAMÍ VELL DEL FAR; **6**; **3h45min**), follow it to the left as it winds towards Albir's promenade, always keeping right until you come to a T-junction with the main road in **Albir**, by all the cafés and bars. Cross the road and turn right for about 150m/yds, to the BUS STOP (**7**; **4h**). Buses to Benidorm run about every 15 minutes.

Walk 6: SERPIS GORGE

See also photos on pages 26, 63
Distance: 20km/12.4mi; 5h
Grade: ● easy, level, out-and-back walk along the route of an old railway line. Fairly long, but you can turn back whenever you like. Some tunnels. Yellow/white PR-CV 207 waymarking
Equipment: see page 42; *plus torch*
How to get there and return: ⛟ to L'Orxa (the 72km-point on Car tour 2). Just before the bridge over the Serpis River, on the western outskirts of the village, turn left uphill and park at the old station (38° 51.018'N, 0° 19.423'W).
Short walk: Castell de Perputxent. 1km/0.6mi; 40min. ● Easy. Equip-ment as page 42; access as main walk. Climb the steep rocky path about 30m/yds to the right of L'Orxa station to the castle shown on pages 26 and 63 (❼; 20min). Or take the track to the left, then join the path.
Alternative walks
1 Serpis circuit. 14km/8.7mi; 4h. ● Strenuous ascent/descent of 350m/1150ft. Equipment *(torch!)*, access as main walk. Follow the main walk to the 1h38min-point at ❹, then take the signposted path to the right. It winds steeply up through aban-doned terraces and past a waterfall. Before you reach a house (2h), you are directed to the left. Meeting a surfaced track, turn right, then left.

Second dam on the Serpis (1h38min)

Keep to the asphalt past several houses but, just after two houses on the left, turn sharp right at a junction (signposted to L'Orxa). Then, at a large ornate house (Casa Tarsan, a 'ecolodge'), turn right again. Climb steeply to an open area on a crest, where a signposted path (**a**) goes up left to the SUMMIT of **La Safor** (**4**; 2h35min). Keep straight ahead, using the map to follow Walk 7 (in reverse) down to L'Orxa (3h50min).

At the CV701, turn right, back to your car.

2 Longer Serpis circuit. 22km/ 13.6mi; about 6h. ● Strenuous and very long. Follow the main walk to the end of the line (**6**), then return to the fork at (**5**) and go left. Use the map to rise up to the surfaced track below La Safor (**a**) and follow Walk 7 (in reverse) down to L'Orxa. At the CV701, turn right, back to your car.

Thispleasant riverside stroll through the picturesque Serpis Gorge can be enjoyed by anyone. From the level track you can appreciate the marked contrast between the sheer cliffs surrounding the gorge and the gentleness of the river flowing through it. The river valley provides an ideal habitat for wild flowers and birds; allow a full day for picnicking, botanising and birdwatching.

Start the walk from **L'Orxa** STATION (**1**): follow the old railway line below the castle. Just after a bend, alongside a little RUINED ENGINE HOUSE with INFO BOARD (**9min**), ignore a track off to the right (*P*6a); continue through extensive olive terraces to the FIRST OF THE TUNNELS (**2**; **30min**). This is quite long, but soon after entering you can see the other end.

You emerge in a gentle landscape with low trees and, in spring, wild flowers everywhere. The heavily-reeded river banks are alive with the song of Cetti's warblers in spring and summer, and crag martins swoop hither and thither as they catch their food on the wing. Fish, some of them unbelievably large, swim unconcernedly in the clear water, and grey herons feed well.

At **46min** a path goes off right to a dam (*P*6b) — the source of the *canaleta* that runs along to the rather grand old hydro-electric station on the opposite side of the river (as you approach it, you will see and hear water cascading down a channel from the *canaleta* above). Leave the track at **1h14min**: go down towards the river and cross it on a low BRIDGE. Just past the chained entrance to the old HYDROELECTRIC STATION (now a water quality control station), take a small path up to a pretty, ruined *ermita* (**3**).

Continue along the track, the river now on your left. You rejoin the railway line at an old ruined BRIDGE

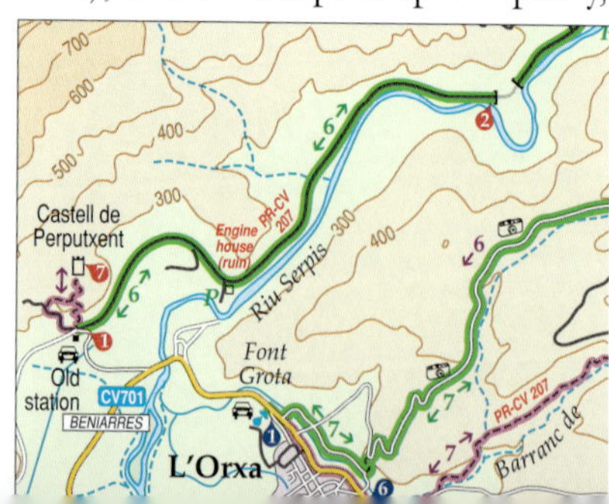

(**1h23min**), where it used to cross the river. Lush orange groves lie between you and the river, before you go through a very short TUNNEL (**1h28min**). After two houses, and just opposite the DAM shown on page 59, note a WALKERS' SIGNPOST indicating a steep path up to the right (**❹**; **1h38min**; *route of Alternative walk 1*). Continue straight ahead here, through the next TUNNEL (**1h41min**) — not much more than a wide arch. Soon you will reach a BRIDGE over an open grassy area (**1h49min**) with paths down to the river — an obvious spot for a break.

Then continue along the track and through a cutting. There are more orange groves down by the river and another *canaleta* runs along the opposite bank. Negotiate another, fairly long TUNNEL (**1h55min**). The LAST OF THE TUNNELS (**2h05min**) is the longest (500m/0.3mi), but can be avoided: just before the entrance, scramble a couple of metres/yards down the slope to the left, then walk along a narrow path to the far end. You will pass a ruined building, another old HYDROELECTRIC STATION, on the river bank before rejoining the railway line (**2h14min**).

When you come to a FORK (**❺**), keep left (*Alternative walk 2 turns left here on the return*). Now high above the river, follow the railway through pine woods, until you come to the end of the line — another dismantled BRIDGE (**❻**; **2h30min**). Standing on top of the old supports, you have a glorious view of the amphitheatre created by the high, rugged peaks and sheer cliffs of La Safor. Now retrace your steps to **L'Orxa** STATION (**❶**; **5h**).

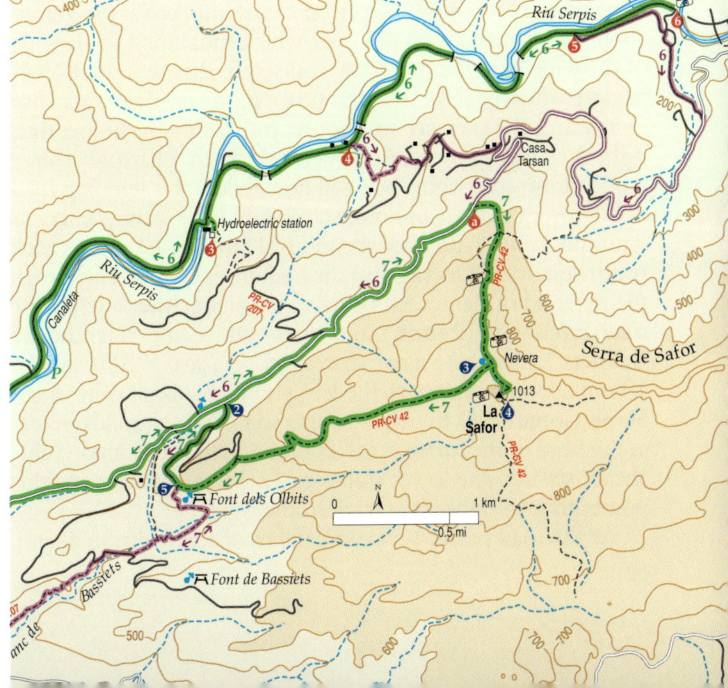

See map pages 60-61
Distance: 15.7km/9.7mi; 5h20min
Grade: ● fairly strenuous, with an ascent and corresponding descent of 765m/2500ft. Paths are good and navigation straightforward; well waymarked with yellow/white PR flashes (PR-CV 42 and 207).
Equipment: see page 42; also compass and long trousers
How to get there and return: ♙ to L'Orxa (the 72km-point on Car tour 2). Shortly after crossing the Serpis River, on the western outskirts of the village, park on the right at the Font Grota — alongside a small garden with stone tables (38° 50.835'N, 0° 18.804'W).
Short walk: L'Orxa — Font dels Olbits — L'Orxa. 7km/4.3mi; 2h20min. ● Easy climb and descent

of 290m/950ft. Equipment as page 42; access as main walk. Follow the main walk to (**2**), then take the track on the right to the **Font dels Olbits** (**5**). Return the same way.
Alternative ascent (or descent) via the Barranc del Bassiet. ● Distance/time/access as main walk, but only recomended for experienced walkers (loose stones underfoot; navigation less straightforward). Leave the Font Grota but do not cross the road. Follow it south for 600m/yds to where it bends right, then fork left on a track behind some recycling bins (**6**; walkers' information board for the PR-CV 207). Some 350m along, descend steps on the left to continue. Follow the path to the **Font dels Olbits** (**5**), then use the map to rejoin the main walk.

Approaching from the west, La Safor looks fairly gentle but, from the north, its jagged peaks and sheer cliffs present quite a different spectacle. Its ascent offers a variety of experiences and scenery. Just below the summit there is a *nevera* and, on the way down, you can take a relaxing break at the picturesque Font dels Olbits.

Start out at the **Font Grota** (**1**): cross the road at the roundabout and turn right on the track which runs along the far side of the wide old river bed, now concreted. Pass two small footbridges; after the second, continue for 65m/yds, then walk 15m up towards the entrance to a house. Just before the house, turn right up a zigzag footpath. When you reach a narrow asphalt road (**6min**) turn right. You will now follow this winding road uphill for more than an hour, so relax and enjoy the scenery as it unfolds around successive bends. In **15min**, you can look back southwest over L'Orxa against the backdrop of Montcabrer, with the pyramid of Benicadell rising to the right. After a while the road levels out (**24min**) and skirts above the **Barranc de Bassiets** (*Alternative ascent/descent on the PR-CV 207*). About 10 minutes later, down to the left, you have a brief view of the Serpis Gorge (Walk 6). After passing some large almond terraces at the head of the *barranc*, the Font dels Olbits becomes visible ahead, set into the lower slopes of La Safor (**46min**). At this point ignore a signposted track to the right.

As the road passes between patches of well-cultivated land,

While at L'Orxa visit the old station (where Walk 6 begins) and the Castell de Perputxtent above it.

watch for a huge galvanised iron WATER TANK on the left (**1h**). About 200m/yds further on, a track to the right leads to the Font dels Olbits. We visit it on the return from La Safor, *but the Short walk turns right here.* Continue along the road. Ignore a concreted track going down into the valley to the left (**1h15min**).

You come to an open area on the left (❶; **1h35min**; *Alternative walks 6-1 and 6-2 join here*). The steep, PR-CV 42-signposted path to 'CIM DE LA SAFOR' heads up the ridge to your right. It is well-trodden, but you will find long trousers handy if the lacerating scrub has not been cut back. As you ascend, take careful note when you reach some CRAGS (**1h50min**) that your path splits into two. Both forks go to the same place. The paths rejoin (**2h 20min**) and, shortly after, you enjoy a magnificent view of the broad amphitheatre formed by the northern face of La Safor. Nearby, the 'eye of the needle' — a natural rock arch — frames another view, down over the coastal plain.

Continue the ascent and reach a flat grassy 'MEADOW' just below the summit (**2h50min**). Here you can investigate the remains of an underground *nevera* (❸; SNOW WELL), before the final, 10-minute ascent up the obvious path to the cross and TRIG POINT on **La Safor** (❹; 1013m/ 3325ft; **3h**). From this summit much of the Costa Blanca is visible below. Ahead, the plain spreads out its blanket of cultivation. To the northeast lies Gandía and the high-rise developments of the *platjas;* the River Serpis (Walk 6) flows in the north. The western skyline is pierced by the distinctive peak of Benicadell. The reservoir at Beniarrés glimmers in the southwest, while the Vall de Gallinera spreads across the southern front, with the massed ranks of the serras of Alicante beyond it. Finally, Montgó (Walk 1) rises to the southeast, with Dénia and Xàbia at its feet.

Retrace your steps to the meadow and take care here to locate the correct path for the descent. Go along the meadow to the left (southwest). The main path at the end of the meadow goes straight ahead, but leads only into difficult terrain with some deep potholes. Your path goes to the right just before entering the trees — be sure to find the clear YELLOW AND WHITE

WAYMARKS. From this point, the route down is clear. Follow the waymarked path, fairly level at first, but gradually getting steeper as it descends. At **3h55min** note a walkers' signpost and a track to the right — a short cut back to your outward route. But take the path ahead to the **Font dels Olbits** (❺; **4h05min**).

Beyond the *font*, you have two options. You can take the track leading round the benches, to rejoin your outward track near the large iron water tank, and turn left. Alternatively, you could take the signposted PR-CV 207 down into the Barranc de Bassiets — an often skiddy descent requiring agility. Whichever option you take, you should be back at the **Font Grota** (❶) by **5h20min**.

View from the Font dels Olbits. The area around the font (which has a year-round water supply), has been beautifully restored, with benches and tables from where you can enjoy this magnificent landscape. Terraces, now largely unexploited, cover the low hills, while Benicadell, sometimes likened to the Matterhorn, rises in the distance.

Walk 8: BARRANC DE LA ENCANTADA AND ERMITA DE SANTO CRISTO

Distance: 10km/6.2mi; 2h55min
Grade: ● moderate, but the climbs up to the *ermita* is quite strenuous. Paths and tracks are good; navigation is straightforward.
Equipment: see page 42
How to get there and return: 🚗 to/from the (signed) Pont de les Calderes, on the CV700 between Muro and Pego (the 53km-point on Car tour 2). Park well off the road, just to the west of the bridge, on the road down to the Barranc de la Encantada (where there is a car park; 38° 47.237'N, 0° 19.322'W). No bus service

Short walk: Barranc de la Encantada. 4km/2.5mi; 1h16min. ● Easy. Equipment and access as above. Follow the main walk to the mill (❹; 38min) and return the same way.

Alternative return: ● At the 2h11min-point turn left on the metalled road (❽), to the modern white house on the saddle. Then take a path off left 100m/yds before the house, back down to your outgoing route near Villa Mónica (ⓐ) — or continue ahead to rejoin the main walk (see map).

In addition to exceptional views, this delightful walk offers a peaceful stroll by a stream, deep pools under the imposing cliffs of an impressive gorge, an optional detour to Planes with its ancient aqueduct and Moorish castle, and an old pilgrimage trail to an *ermita*. Autumn, when the heather is purple on the hillsides and trees in the valleys shine yellow and gold, is the best time of year.

Begin the walk at the CAR PARK on the Barranc de la Encantada road west of the **Pont de les Calderes** (❶): follow the lane downhill. Descending slightly through orchards, it leads to a ruin (**10min**) and your first glimpse of water in the **Barranc de la Encantada** on the right. A little further on, you pass a ford across the watercourse, and the cliffs of the gorge begin to appear. The sound of running water accompanies you, as the gorge becomes deeper. In **15min** wooden steps beckon you down to the first of the pools, but only a minute ahead, at the **Gorg del Salt** (❷), are the steps to the main POOLS (*P*8a). You'll see a lot of cars parked here. Calcium salts give the water a green and cloudy look, but it is fresh and cool.

Continue along the road and, as you leave this narrow section of gorge, terracing opens out around you. The Serra de la Albureca appears ahead, while to the right are the rugged crags of the Serra de Foradá. When the road bends right and descends steeply down into the valley, turn off left on a forestry track and pass the black gates of VILLA MÓNICA (**24min**). Then take the path to the right and descend through a small orchard; the path leads you beside a stream running through small green fields. Ignore a path going uphill to the left (ⓐ; *the Alternative return descends this path*) as your path goes along the edge of a ploughed

From the heights above the Barranc de la Encantada, there is a magnificent view of the church at Beniarrés, standing proud above the village. The Serra de Benicadell fills in the background.

field. You come upon pools, a tiny RESERVOIR (*P*8b) and another ruined *casita* (❸; **31min**). More rugged peaks are visible ahead as the gorge closes in.

This is a popular walk so several paths have been created. As long as you keep the *barranc* on your right, you can take whichever you wish — they all lead to the **Moli de l'Encantada** (❹; **38min**), where the *barranc* becomes very deep and sheer. *The Short walk turns back here.*

The path climbs up to the left then levels out near the top of the cliff, with views down the remainder of the *barranc* to the Serpis River (**51min**). Continue upwards through olive terraces to a small building. Walk past the gate at the right of the building (the fruit on the trees just below the gate, bright orange when ripe, is persimmon). Continue through the remainder of the terraces and turn left on the surfaced road you meet at the ridge (❺; **1h01min**). But first spend a few minutes taking in the fantastic views below — the upper Serpis Valley, the Embalse de Beniarrés, and the magnificent Serra de Benicadell almost straight ahead. Walk down the road in the setting shown above; VILLA ISABELITA (**1h09min**) commands the sort of views that most of us can only dream about.

At **1h33min** the village of Planes comes into view.* As you meet the asphalt road, turn left; after about 200m/yds (just past

---

*You can make a (highly recommended) detour into Planes at the 1h38min-point: pass the steps and continue down the road for 200m/yds, then take the road to the right. Cross the *barranc* and keep uphill to the font (still in use) and the aqueduct (10min). From here you can easily see your way through the village to the Moorish castle (10min). After the detour return to the steps to continue.

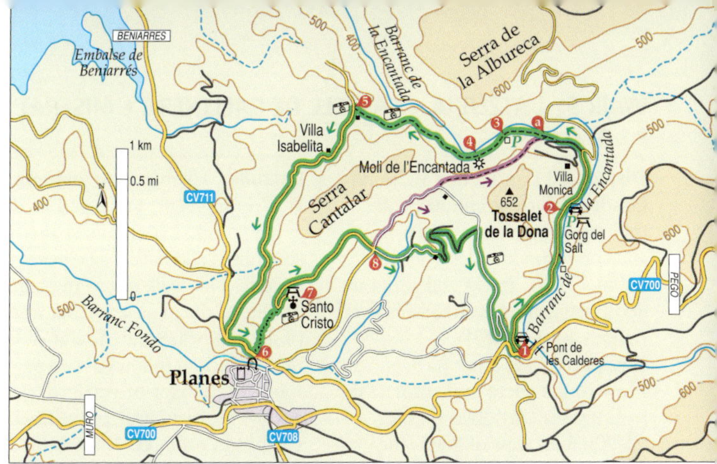

the 1km marker), take STEPS up left (**6**; **1h38min**) towards the Ermita del Santo Cristo. The first few steps are concrete, but the rest are hewn out of natural rock and make for an easy, though strenuous, ascent. Take it slowly, admire the views and count the STATIONS OF THE CROSS as you go. The twelfth station appears at **2h**, as you meet the road which winds round the back of the hill from Planes. There is a thirteenth station just before the entrance to the **Ermita del Santo Cristo** (**7**; **2h01min**), where you will also find picnic benches and fantastic views.

Leave the *ermita* by heading downhill on the asphalt road. The Embalse de Beniarrés sparkles below and, if you are lucky, you may see Bonelli's eagles soaring above. They are resident in this area of Spain, and their white bodies and darker wings make them identifiable with the naked eye. At the crossroads (**8**; **2h11min**) go straight ahead on a surfaced track *(but left for the Alternative return)*, walking through mixed fruit orchards down into and across a *barranc*. Ignore all tracks going off into terraces; keep to the main track, which eventually loses the tarred surface and zigzags quite sharply uphill.

At **2h26min** a modern white house comes into view on the saddle (on the route of the Alternative return), and you meet another fork. This time take the track which climbs to the right. When it levels out, you can almost see down the Barranc de la Encantada again (behind a house on the left). A minute later, as you meet another track (**2h36min**), turn right. This surfaced track descends along a heather-clad ridge, with the Barranc de la Encantada on the left and views over to the *ermita* and Planes on your right, providing a wonderful overview of the countryside traversed throughout the walk. The track takes you all the way back to your PARKING PLACE near the **Pont de les Calderes** (**1**; **2h55min**).

Walk 9: L'ATZUBIA • CASTELL DE GALLINERA • MISERAT • L'ATZUBIA

Distance: 11km/6.8mi; 3h20min
Grade: ● fairly strenuous, with prolonged, sometimes steep, ascents and corresponding descents of 540m/1770ft. Tracks and paths are good; navigation is straightforward (mostly PR-CV 58.4).
Equipment: see page 42
How to get there and return: 🚗 to L'Atzubia (Adsubia) on the CV700 5km west of Pego (the 97km-point on Car tour 2); follow 'Centre urbà' to park in the tiny square (38° 50.837'N, 0° 9.049'W).
Short walks: Gallinera Castle. ●
Fairly strenuous ascent/descent of 300m/980ft. Equipment, access as main walk. Follow the main walk to the first saddle and back (fine view of the castle; 5.5km/3.4mi; 1h45min) or go to the saddle below the castle and back (❹; 7km/4.3mi; 2h15min).
Alternative walk: L'Atzubia — Castell de Gallinera — Miserat — L'Atzubia. 10km/6.2mi; 2h45min.
● ‼ Equipment, access and grade as main walk, but you must also be surefooted and have a head for heights. This walk covers the same ground as the main walk, but instead of skirting below the Miserat cliffs on the track, it follows a narrow footpath (**danger of vertigo**). Follow the main walk to the track by Gallinera Castle (❹; 1h06min), where the main walk turns left. Here take the waymarked path between the track and your outward path (still the PR-CV 58.4). This narrow and rocky path, clearly marked, leads under the northern cliffs of Miserat. It crosses a few short screes horizontally, and leads to a track after about 30min (there may be some beehives here). Turn right on the track. On reaching an asphalt road, turn left and pick up the main walk at the 2h14min-point (❻; notes on page 72).

This walk takes you through rural countryside, ascends an old mule trail, contours under imposing cliffs, and offers unbelievable views of one of the region's strategically-sited castles. Birdwatchers and botanists will find much to interest them in this varied terrain.

The walk starts by the *font* in the tiny MAIN SQUARE in L'Atzubia (❶). Climb CARRER PRINCIPAL past the CHURCH to where it ends by a CROSS. Then take the middle road, which bears slightly left. Despite being surfaced, this road sees little traffic. It takes you through the orange groves at the beginnings of the very fertile Gallinera Valley and alongside the Barranc de Michel down to your left. All the time you will be climbing steadily, so take it slowly and enjoy the pleasant country atmosphere. Ahead you can see the Castell de Gallinera and higher up, to its left, the TV antennas on top of Miserat. Even further to the left, your return route is visible, snaking down the hillside. Ignore a road off to the left (**10min**) and start climbing a little more steeply.

At **18min**, as you go under the electricity lines, make sure to follow the road round a hairpin to the left, ignoring the track going straight ahead. Many of the terraces around here are

On the approach to Gallinera Castle, 1h into the walk. You can take a 20min return detour to the castle, but it is privately owned and kept locked.

cultivated with *algarrobas* — carob or locust beans; they are used for animal feed. Nowadays, however, this crop is less popular and rarely seen. The road zigzags up towards an obvious saddle below Miserat, and you will have passed a RESERVOIR and a few houses by the time it becomes a track (**29min**). It then winds steadily up the lower slopes of Miserat, its antennas still visible above. The orange groves have been left far below; only carobs, olives and almonds grace these higher slopes.

Looking back as you contour along one of the flatter sections, there is a good view of L'Atzubia, framed in the hills, with the coastal plain and the sea behind it. At a Y-fork (**❷; 35min**) go uphill to the right. The wide track bends round to the left, but be sure to follow it in a hairpin bend to the right at the next fork, 500m/yds further on (**❸; 46min**), ignoring a track straight ahead. Pass in front of a house and continue on what is now just an old narrow mule trail which zigzags up over the terraces. Following the PR markers, you reach a FIRST SADDLE (**53min**), from where there is a superb view of Gallinera Castle. *The first Short walk option turns back here.*

From the saddle you can pick out the next part of your route going round the slopes towards the castle. The well-marked path is level at first, then it climbs through some old almond terraces. You pass to the left of a ruined *casita,* before levelling out a bit under a crag and joining a track on another SADDLE just below the **Castell de Gallinera** (**❹; 1h06min**), from where you will have the view of the castle shown in the photo above. (This track goes all the way down into the valley, to the village of Benirrama, which claims the castle as its own and calls it Castell de Benirrama.) *The second Short walk turns back here.*

Turn left on the track, to circle under the imposing cliffs of **Miserat**. *(The path here, lying between your upward route and the track you are now following, is the continuation of the PR-CV 58.4 and the route of the Alternative walk.)* As you set off on this new track, you have a magnificent view of the entire Gallinera Valley below to the right. The track is initially wide, but in very poor condition — rocky, or just stony, and deeply furrowed by running water; the presence of several large boulders indicates the instability of the cliffs above. As you proceed, the track deteriorates further — at times it is little more than a footpath. Your views of the castle, however, continue to improve!

Ignore paths off to the terraces and continue uphill beneath the cliffs, which are home to peregrine falcons and ravens. As you approach the plateau below Miserat, the landscape opens out, heralding a change in bird life — look out for black redstart, goldfinch and wheatear.

At **1h45min** you are on the wide plateau which stretches between Vall de Gallinera and Vall d'Ebo and, if it is a Sunday or a *fiesta* in autumn, you may spot a number of *seta* (wild mushroom) gatherers foraging hopefully in the vegetation, baskets or buckets hanging over their arms.

At **1h53min** join a narrow surfaced road and turn left. At the top of the hill (**5**; **2h**) the energetic may like to turn left and climb the road to the SUMMIT OF **Miserat** (**a**; 757m/2480ft). But the main walk heads downhill to the right here, with Pego visible just beyond the valley below, and the coast clear in the distance.

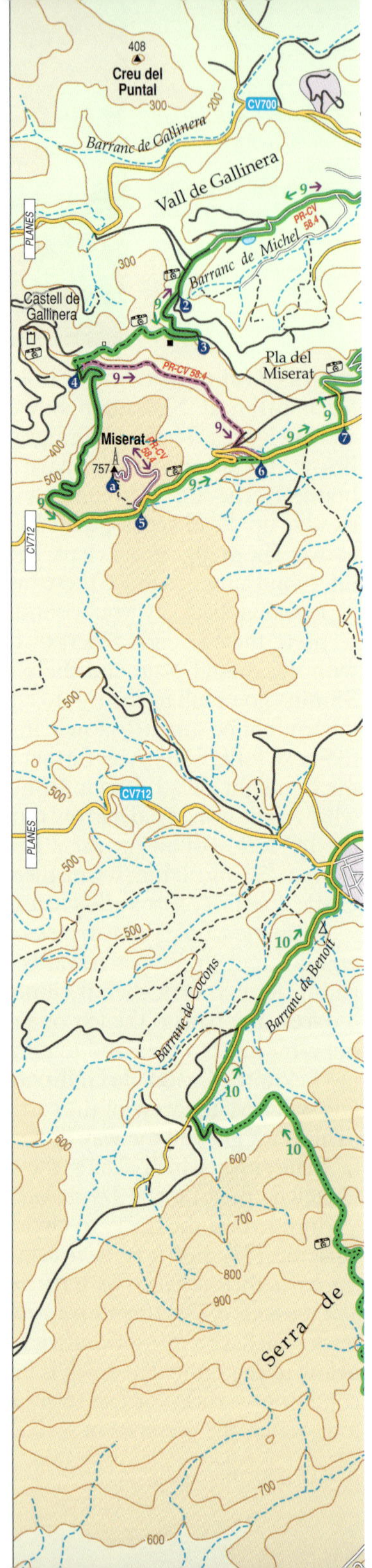

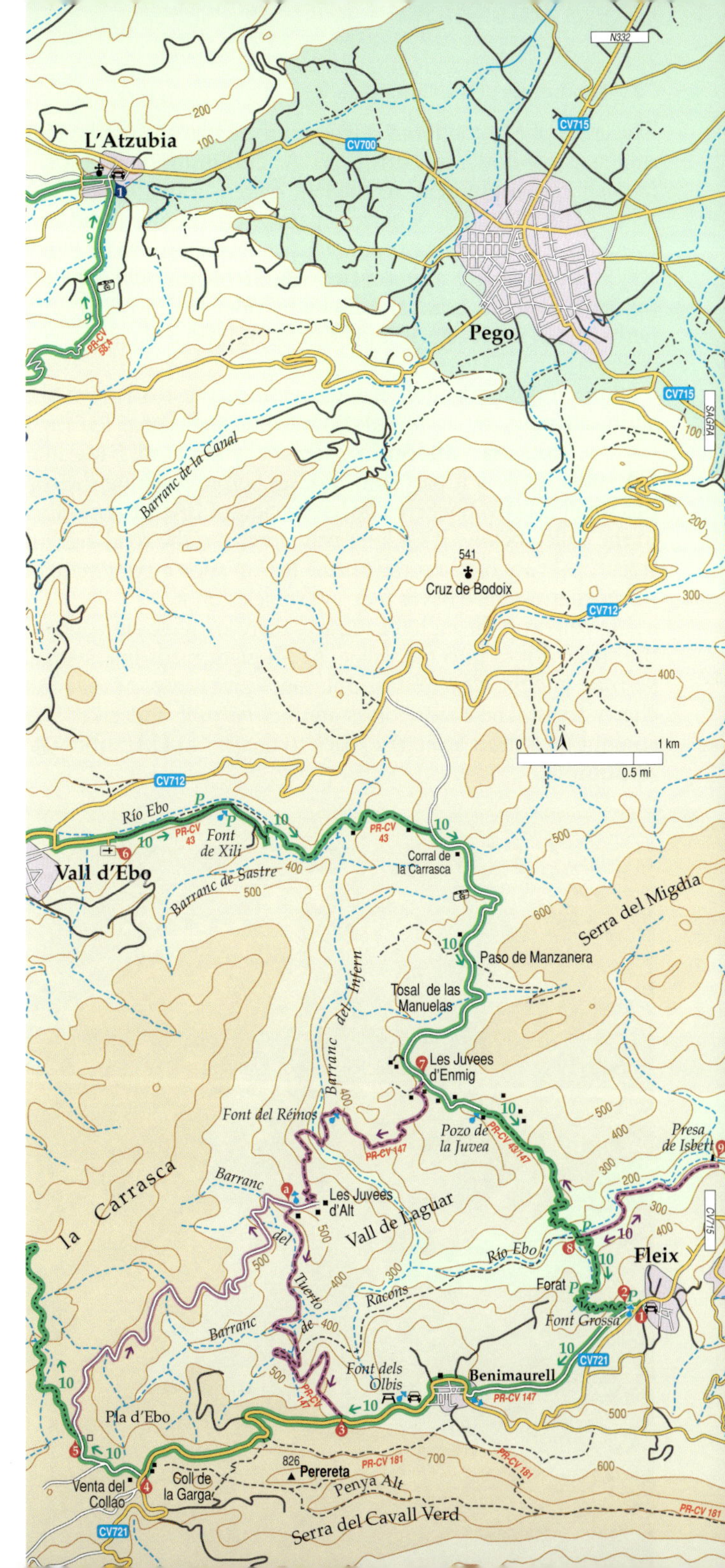
N332
CV700
CV715
L'Atzubia
9
9
PR-CV 55.4
Pego
CV715
SAGRA
200
100
100
200
300
Barranc de la Canal
541
Cruz de Bodoix
CV712
400
N
0
1 km
0.5 mi
CV712
Río Ebo
P
P
10
PR-CV 43
10
10
PR-CV 43
Font de Xili
Vall d'Ebo
6
Corral de la Carrasca
Barranc de Sastre
400
500
500
600
Serra del Migdia
10
Paso de Manzanera
Tosal de las Manuelas
Barranc del Infern
400
Les Juvees d'Enmig
7
10
PR-CV 43/147
500
400
300
Presa de Isbert
9
Font del Réinos
PR-CV 147
Pozo de la Juvea
200
300
400
CV715
la Carrasca
Barranc
a
Les Juvees d'Alt
500
Vall de Laguar
Río Ebo
P
8
10
Fleix
del
400
300
Racons
Forat
P
2
P
1
Font Grossa
Tuerto
Barranc
de
400
500
Font dels Olbis
Benimaurell
PR-CV 147
10
CV721
500
10
de
500
PR-CV 147
3
Pla d'Ebo
5
10
826
Perereta
PR-CV 181
700
600
Venta del Collao
4
Coll de la Garga
Penya Alt
PR-CV 181
Serra del Cavall Verd
CV721

The crags of Miserat loom starkly on the left as the road winds quite steeply down towards Pego. At **2h09min**, on a particularly sharp hairpin bend to the left, there is a small open area with a large boulder. A narrow path goes straight ahead and provides a fragrant short-cut which avoids that long bend. Rejoin the road five minutes later (**❻**; **2h14min**); *the Alternative walk comes in here*. The rocky hillsides are carpeted with herbs, dwarf palms, gorse and heather, and you will pass several *casitas*.

Some 600m/yds after having rejoined the road from the short-cut path, by a FIRE RISK WARNING SIGN, turn left on a narrow road (**❼**; **2h23min**). This is your road back into L'Atzubia. Follow it past some houses before reaching the top of a small rise, from where you have a view of L'Atzubia nestling in the valley below. It's a long way down, so the road zigzags steeply — very hard on the knees! It is in such a poor state of repair that we have never met any vehicles on it.

As you drop through the terraces there are wide views down the sheer slopes into the valley. At **3h** giant reeds line a small *barranc,* and the *algarrobas* and almonds give way to orange and cherry trees. The road crosses another *barranc* and takes you straight up a short steep rise, back to the *font* in **L'Atzubia** (**❶**; **3h20min**).

Walk 10: SERRA DE LA CARRASCA AND THE MOZARABIC TRAILS

See map on pages 70-71; see also photo on page 12

Distance: 23km/14.3mi; 6h50min

Grade: ● long and strenuous, with ascents/descents of 900m/2950ft. Beyond the Venta del Collao the walk is no longer maintained/waymarked; other stretches require careful navigation. *Only suitable for experienced walkers and only in cool weather.*

Equipment: see page 42; also *GPS/ compass,* towel, picnic, plenty of water

How to get there and return: 🚍 to Fleix (the 122km-point on Car tour 1); park near the school, in a car park at the western end of Fleix, facing two walkers' information boards (38° 46.695'N, 0° 6.607'W).

Short walk: Mozarabic trail. 2.5km/1.5mi; 1h10min. ● Easy descent/tiring re-ascent of 180m/ 590ft. Equipment, access as *Alternative walk 1.* Follow *Alternative walk 1* to the falls (30min) and retrace steps.

Alternative walks

1 Embalse de Isbert. 5.5km/3.4mi; 2h40min. ● Strenuous descent/re-ascent of 260m/850ft. In summer, the bed of the Río Ebo is a furnace; do *not* attempt this outside the cool season. Access and equipment as main walk (except compass). Follow the main walk to the *lavadero* (5min; *P*10b), then take the path down to the right 30m/yds further on (❷) — the beginning of the MOZARABIC TRAIL shown below. Descend through a ROCK ARCH (*forat*) to the base of a (seasonal) WATERFALL (30min; *P*10c) and continue down to the pebbly river bed (❽; 45min; *P*10d). Turn right and wind downstream through this amazing gorge to the **Presa de Isbert** (❾; 1h15min). Most of the year this reservoir is completely dry — hence its popular name, 'Isbert's Folly'. Return the same way.

The Mozarabic trail, seen from the rock arch (6h15min into the main walk, but only 25min from Fleix; Alternative walk 1 and Picnics 10c-d). The word 'Mozarabic ('would-be Arab') refers to Christians who were allowed to practise their religion under Moorish rule. To get around in the mountainous terrain they built narrow trails which were cleverly stepped so that the usual difficulties associated with steep ascents and descents were minimised. Natural rock was used where possible, but for the most part they represent a remarkable feat of design and construction. Some have since fallen into disrepair and others have been lost to vegetation, sometimes coming to light by chance or after a severe fire. But many remain in good order today and are followed in this book.

2 Barranc del Infern and a Mozarabic trail. 10km/6.2mi; 3h. ●
Strenuous, with ascents/descents of about 500m/1650ft. Park at the Font d'els Olbis on the CV721 west of Fleix (**❸**; 38° 46.284'N, 0° 8.059'W). Follow the main walk from the 43min-point to the 1h24min-point (**❺**), then keep on the unmade road — to the abandoned houses of **Juvees d'Alt** (**ⓐ**; Upper Juvees). Just before a ruined house, at a signpost 'Font dels Olbis', turn right on the yellow/white waymarked PR-CV 147. You descend via the **Barranc del Tuerto** to the **Barranc de Racons**, where Mozarabic steps come underfoot. Where a path comes in from the left, go straight on for 'Benimaurell', back to the CV721 at (**❸**), where you turn left to the Font dels Olbis.

3 Barranc del Infern and Mozarabic trails (PR-CV 147). 14.5km/ 9mi; 5h. ● Strenuous; ascents/descents of about 900m/1950ft overall; access as main walk. Follow *Alternative walk 1* to the river bed (**❽**), then continue up the far side on the PR-CV 147.

When you meet an unmade road at the **Pozo de la Juvea**, follow it to a signpost 'Juvees d'Enmig' (**❼**; Middle Juvees). Turn left here on a footpath. The path passes to the left of a house and runs downhill through terracing before coming to the **Font del Réinos**. Slither down to the river bed, where another sign directs you up to **Juvees d'Alt** (**ⓐ**; Upper Juvees). Turn right on the unmade road here for 200m/yds, passing a well on the right. Just past a ruined house on the left, the PR-CV 147 is signposted left to the Font dels Olbis. You descend via the **Barranc del Tuerto** to the **Barranc de Racons**, where more MOZARABIC STEPS come underfoot. Where a path comes in from the left, continue straight ahead for 'Benimaurell', back to the CV721 at (**❸**), where you turn left past the **Font dels Olbis** to Benimaurell. Keep to the CV721 past a large restaurant and the village car park (left), then fork left downhill on a rough road. Follow this back to your car in Fleix (**❶**).

I f you are fit enough to tackle a really long, full-day walk, then do not miss some version of this one. The main walk takes you along the Vall de Laguar, over the barren Carrasca Ridge and into Vall d'Ebo for a break in one of the bars. After crossing the Barranc del Infern, you return on a pair of Mozarabic trails, one plunging steeply down into the bed of the Ebo, the other thrusting back up again. But if you prefer not to walk cross-country without waymarks, the alternative walks are no less exhilarating.

Begin at the PARKING AREA in **Fleix** (**❶**): continue west along the road (YELLOW/WHITE WAYMARKS, PR-CV 147). Almost immediately, take the rough road to the right. Pass **Font Grossa** and the village WASHHOUSE shown on page 12 (**5min**; *P*10b). Some 50m further on, the path down to the right (**❷**) is your return route. *(Turn down right here for Alternative walks 1 and 3 or P10c, d.)* Continue winding gently up through almond groves, past another *font* and *lavadero*. Climb steeply into **Benimaurell** (**29min**) and keep right to circle the village to the north. Pass the car park and a large restaurant on the right, then bear left and fork right three times, to leave the village on the CV721.

As you gain height, notice the Serra del Cavall Verd on the left, the Barranc del Infern on the right and the barren Carrasca Ridge ahead. After passing the **Font dels Olbis** on the right (**43min**), then a path with info board for the PR-CV 147 down right at (**3**), continue to the **Venta del Collao** (**4**; **1h13min**). Turn right here on a track, ignoring the fingerposts just at the right of the restaurant. The main walk now heads up to Carrasca, the ridge which looms ahead to your right. Ignore a track to the left (**1h18min**) and continue down to a SADDLE (**5**; **1h24min**) at the head of two valleys: on the right, running northeast, is the Vall de Laguar; on the left, running southwest, is the beginning of the Jalón Valley. You will be heading, *pathless,* for the small saddle ahead, at the top of the Carrasca Ridge.

Head left off the track here, making a beeline for the saddle (350°). *(But for Alternative walk 2, keep ahead on the track.)* Sadly, this stretch is no longer waymarked, but you should reach the SADDLE at the top of **Carrasca Ridge** in about **2h05min**. Vall d'Ebo is far below, and you can see along the coast from Dénia to Gandía. The summit of Miserat, with its TV antenna, is across the valley on the Gallinera Ridge. On the same line of sight, but only about 20m/yds ahead, is the continuation of your route.

You want to be contouring to the right about 20m/yds below the top of the ridge — heading northeast — up and round the left side of the rocky hillock about 500m away. So just make your way to the left slope of the hillock (**2h13min**), beyond which you see Miserat and the TV antenna. From here walk down the wide flat ridge, heading west of north and keeping Miserat ahead to the right. The village of Vall d'Ebo can be seen below, slightly to the right of the direction in which you are walking (**2h18min**). This spur will take you all the way down off the mountain.

The terrain makes for easy walking, but take care when the descent becomes a little steeper, with *barrancs* on either side. To the left of Vall d'Ebo village you'll see a *finca* with a red-tiled roof; in front of it there is a little stone shelter surrounded by extensive almond and olive terraces. Make your way down to the top TERRACE (**2h39min**), then circle left and downhill through the terraces to the SHELTER. From here, locate another small building on the opposite side of a *barranc* and contour round to it (**2h55min**). Pass just to the right of this building and continue round the groves, skirting to the left of a small hillock, until you reach a farm track just below. Turn right towards a *finca* and reach an asphalt road (**3h04min**). Follow it downhill to the right, into **Vall d'Ebo** (**3h20min**).

Refreshment is available in the village*, but if you have a picnic, press on. Past the SPORTS CENTRE and CAMPSITE, turn left to a BRIDGE OVER THE **Ebo** (**3h23min**). Don't cross it; turn right along the river. At the next BRIDGE, turn right, away from the bridge, then turn sharp left on the waymarked PR-CV 43. Continue along the river, past the CEMETERY on your right (**❻**; **3h33min**). A track takes you past a FORD, to a junction (**3h39min**). If water is flowing, there is a good picnic spot by the river five minutes along the left fork (*P*10a). We head *right* here (signposted 'Vall de Laguar'), to **Font de Xili** (**3h44min**), another setting for *P*10a.

From Font de Xili the track continues high above the bed of the **Barranc del Infern**. Watch out on the left for the *clear, waymarked* PR-CV 43 path down to the river bed (about six minutes or 550m/yds from the *font* at time of writing, but it may be re-routed) — *be sure to locate the waymarks!* After crossing the river bed (**3h58min**), the path climbs for a few minutes, then begins to descend again. This section can be eroded in places. On reaching an ABANDONED ALMOND GROVE (**4h05min**) the path goes up to the right, climbing very steeply past a RUINED HOUSE. Turning sharp left after the house, the path continues rising through scrub to another almond grove and then a newer HOUSE (**4h20min**). Join the track leading from this house and meet an unmade road after a further 200m/yds. Turn right; the road takes you around the head of a *barranc*, past a crumbling house on the right, with a WELL (**Corral de la Carrasca**; **4h38min**). Soon (**4h44min**) you will spot several buildings on the far side of a little ravine — **Les Juvees d'Enmig** (**❼**; Middle Juvees).

Follow the waymarks past this outpost and to the **Pozo de la Juvea** (**5h10min**), a well with five stone animal troughs. Walk round the well and descend the path to the left of the adjacent house, following a terrace wall. This is the beginning of your long zigzag descent into the bed of the Ebo on the MOZARABIC TRAIL shown on pages 72-73. After a while, look for the twin trail winding up the far side to your final destination, Fleix, and, part-way up, a waterfall — which must be imagined unless there has been heavy rain! Cross the (usually dry) bed of the **Ebo** (**❽**; **5h55min**; *P*10d) and then zigzag up the far side, passing below the seasonal WATERFALL (**6h10min**) and under very steep cliffs (*P*10c). Go through a huge arch cut in the rock by the Mozarabs (*forat*), pass across the top of the waterfall, and stagger up to the top (**6h44min**). Turn left to the *lavadero* and main road, then left again to the PARKING AREA in **Fleix** (**❶**; **6h50min**).

---

*If you have been in the village centre, head east from Plaza Mayor until you reach the *second* (waymarked) bridge in the text.

Walk 11: VUELTA DEL SOMO (SOMO CIRCUIT)

Distance: 11km/6.8mi; 3h19min
Grade: ● easy-moderate, with ascents and corresponding descents of 260m/850ft. Good surfaces underfoot; straightforward navigation with some PR signposting
Equipment: see page 42
How to get there and return: 🚗 from Benidorm: take the CV715 north and turn left just past Tàrbena, on the CV752. About 100m before the 3km marker (the 93km-point on Car tour 3), turn left on a road towards some houses (Casas de Bixauca). Park where the road sweeps left at a ruined house on the right (38° 42.860'N, 0° 7.228'W). No bus service

For variety of terrain, overwhelming views and outstanding scenery, this walk comes near the top of the list. While Somo itself is an unremarkable mountain, as you make this anti-clockwise circuit it becomes obvious why this is one of our favourite walks. Look out for golden eagles which hunt in the area … and for the tracks of the wild boar so prized by hunters.

Start out at the **Casas de Bixauca** (**1**): take the concrete track which goes off the hairpin bend where you parked. You are making for the saddle to the west, where there is an orange stone building, and will then go around the back of Somo, the hill to its left, and return through the valley. Just at the far side of some ruins (**Finca Bixauca; 3min**), there is an open grassy area (**P**11a). But take a path a few metres/yards *before* the picnic spot, going downhill between drystone walls, to a track and

Bolulla Castle rises on a ridge beyond almond groves, just 20min into the walk. To catch the almond trees in blossom, walk in early February. In April, cherry blossom will feature on this walk.

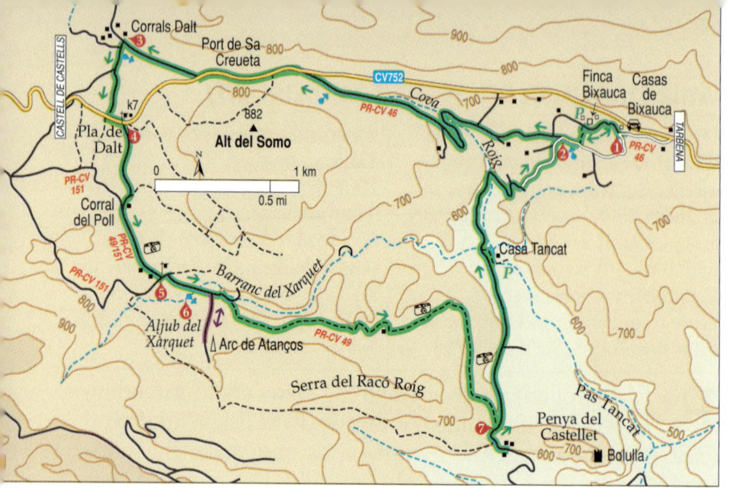

a WELL (**6min**). Turn right and 100m/yds further on, fork right on another track (**❷**; **9min**; your return route is the track on the left). Concreted in places, the track heads west through the almond groves shown on page 77, parallel with the CV752 road.

Ignore a track to the left and another to the right, then cross the **Barranc de la Cova Roig** (**24min**). The track sweeps left and appears to be going in the wrong direction. But it is just gaining height and will soon zigzag round to the west again. At **40min** join a track which enters from the left and climbs gently past a large round WATER TANK to the road (**46min**). Turn left and climb to the saddle you saw earlier — the **Port de Sa Creueta** (also called the **Coll de Bixauca; 54min**), from where the peaks of Serrella rise ahead in the west. Some 500 metres below the col, turn right on a track (**1h**) — a gentle stroll through flat rural countryside. At a junction where there is a collection of houses (**❸**; **Corrals Dalt; 1h09min**), turn left and head directly towards the craggy ridge of Aixorta. Fork left (**1h11min**) past a WELL and reach the road again (**1h15min**). Watch out around here for corn buntings; their rattling call is unmistakable. Cross the road and take the wide track 80 metres to the left (just short of the KM7 MARKER), by an INFORMATION BOARD for the PR-CV 151 (**❹**). You head towards Aixorta. This area, **Pla de Dalt**, is a popular spot for people gathering *setas* (wild mushrooms) in autumn.

The track, signposted 'FONT DELS TEIXOS', climbs gradually past a small pine wood and through almond groves to a house on the right (**1h31min**). Some 50m/yds further on, at a T-JUNCTION (**❺**), go left for 'ALJUB DEL XARQUET'. Ignoring a minor track off left to some ruins, follow the main track downhill into the beginnings of the **Barranc del Xarquet**. Off to the right, in the stony stream bed, is an ancient Moorish well, the **Aljub del Xarquet** (❻; **1h35min**). (Just past the well, you could take a 40min return detour: follow a track on the right. It leads to a point below a rock arch, the Arc de Atanços, from where it is possible to clamber up for a closer look.)

The main walk goes straight ahead here, following the Barranc del Xarquet. As the track sweeps downhill to the left, take a narrow path on the right, edging an almond grove (**1h40min**). You will follow this narrow but clear path (the PR-CV 49, but unsigned when last surveyed) for some time as it skirts around the **Serra del Racó Roig**, with the Barranc del Xarquet deep on the left.

At **1h49min** a huge cave comes into view on the far side of the *barranc*. The path passes a stone shed and rounds some extensive but abandoned terraces (**2h**). Then you climb a rather desolate hillside to a CREST (**2h06min**), from where you enjoy a first good view of the sheer cliffs of the **Pas Tancat** ('Closed Gorge'). Descending southwards, the views encompass the high peaks of the Bernia Ridge to the southeast, Bolulla Castle on its craggy ridge (Penya del Castellet) and the Serra Gelada to the south, close to Benidorm. Across the valley, to the left, you can see your homeward track snaking up to the houses around Finca Bixauca and, on the valley floor, a *finca* which you will reach later in the walk.

The path continues round the Serra del Racó Roig, all the while losing a little height (and perhaps crossing an old rock-fall), until it reaches a SADDLE (❼; **2h30min**), where it meets a wide forestry track coming up from the valley. You will turn down left here, but first go over the saddle and look at the old settlement which locals call 'the high place'. One or two houses are being restored. From the saddle the crags below Bolulla Castle rise impressively above you.

Return to the track and descend. Pas Tancat almost defies belief from this vantage point, so sheer are its cliffs. Ignore a track off right to terraces just before a short uphill section, and continue down to the valley floor. Soon after passing some olive groves a path goes right (**2h53min**) to **Casa Tancat**, the *finca* you saw from above — a perfect spot for a break (**P**11b), surrounded by cherry groves.

From here the track climbs steeply out of the valley and eventually becomes asphalted. Looking back, you can marvel at the terrain you have just crossed. Just beyond some grassy terraces and a shed set amongst pines (**3h13min**), you reach the WELL passed on the outward route. Turn left up the path and then right on the concrete track, back to the **Casas de Bixauca** (❶; **3h19min**).

Walk 12: FONTS DE L'ALGAR • SERRA DE BERNIA • BARRANC DE BINARREAL • FONTS DE L'ALGAR

See also photo on page 23
Distance: 20km/12.4mi; 6h
Grade: ● moderate-strenuous, with ascents and corresponding descents of 440m/1440ft. Good terrain underfoot. Navigation is straight-forward. *After exceptionally heavy rains, the main walk and Alternative walk 2 will be impassable.*
Equipment: see page 42; also long trousers
How to get there and return: 🚗 to/from Casa Federico, Restaurante Bar La Cascada (one of several restaurants in Fonts de l'Algar; after the 159km point on Car tour 1; 38° 39.522'N, 0° 5.875'W). No bus service
Short walk: Algar (or Sacos) Valley. 6km/3.7mi; 2h15min. ● Moderate climb/descent of 120m/395ft. Equipment as page 42. Access as main walk. Follow the main walk to the 32min-point at (❷). Now go straight ahead on the quiet asphalt road which is basically level and gives good views along the Algar Valley and Bernia Ridge. Walk to the end of the asphalt (56min) or the ruined houses (1h10min) and return the same way.
Alternative walks
1   Fonts de l'Algar — Serra de Bérnia — Fonts de l'Algar. 8.5km/5.2mi; 3h. ● Moderate-strenuous, with ascents and corresponding descents of 300m/980ft. Equipment as page 42; access as

main walk. Follow the main walk to the 1h49min-point (❹), then cross the valley and wind uphill to a T-junction where ahead there is a ruined house with outbuildings and about 50m/yds to the left a lovely well. Turn right and almost immediately left onto a track. You have rejoined the main walk at the 4h47min-point (❽).
2   Circuit from Tàrbena. 11km/6.8mi; 3h35min. Moderate; equipment as for main walk. Park at the *mirador* on the CV715 just below Restaurante Sa Cantarella (❶; the 152km-point on Car tour 1; 38° 41.521'N, 0° 5.649'W). Walk a few metres uphill and cross over to take a (poorly) surfaced track that climbs the bank and heads towards the Bernia Ridge. Follow the track to the 'stop' sign, go straight across, and pass to the right of the 'Nexo' building (❼; 9min). Pick up the main walk at the 3h57min-point and follow it to the junction at the 4h47min-point (❽; 59min). Carry on downhill, winding left. The track levels out and crosses the often-dry **Algar (or Sacos) River** at the valley floor (❹; 1h17min). Leave the track as it bears right and take the rocky track off to the left, picking up the main walk after the 1h49min-point. Follow it to the 3h57min-point (❼), where you turn right (3h25min), getting back to your car within ten minutes.

This walk takes you through two fertile valleys, where the varied countryside is quite gentle despite being surrounded by rugged and barren serras. A highlight is the impressive Pas dels Bandolers (Brigands' Pass). Birdwatchers and botanists will find much of interest, particularly in spring, and even if you don't actually see wild boar you will notice evidence of their presence.

Start out in the CAR PARK at **Casa Federico** (❶). Go along

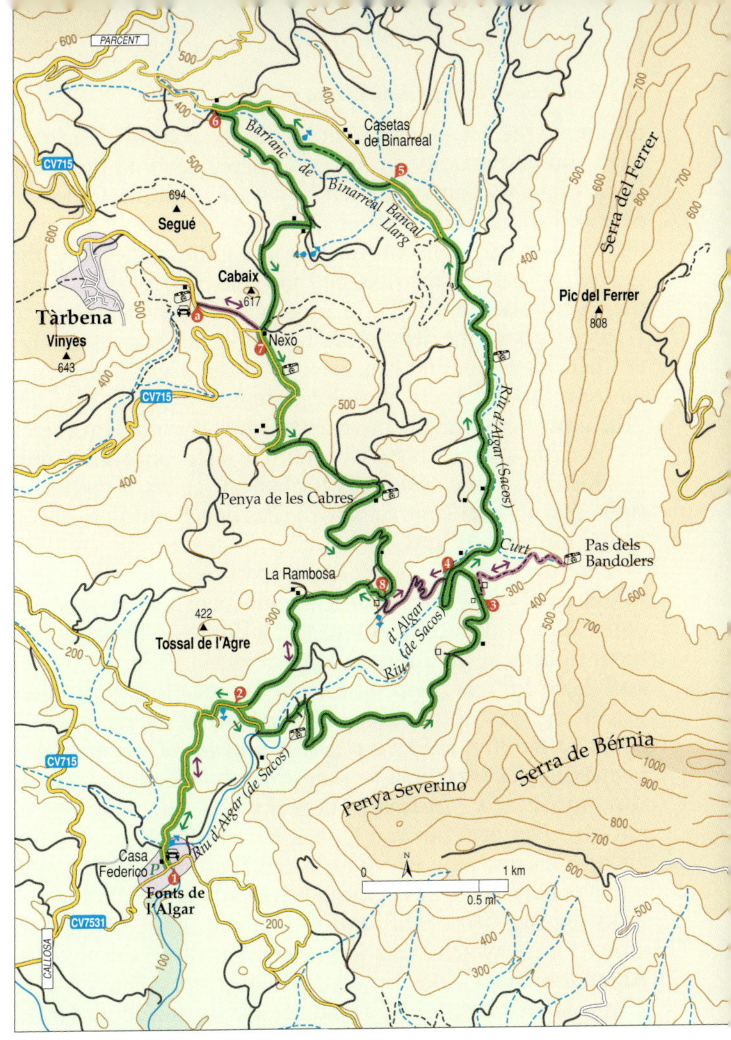

by the water, past two small WATERFALLS (*P*12; photo on page 23) and into a narrow asphalt road. This road bears right (**3min**) and starts to climb very steeply. Ignore tracks to groves of oranges and *nísperos* (medlars) or houses and continue up to the TOP OF THE RISE (**21min**). From here the road is almost level. As you stop for a breather, look back to Campana, Ponoch, Aitana and Aixorta. Penya Severino (the end of the Serra de Bernia) and Ferrer rise to the right, their cliffs separated by a narrow vertical gap — the Pas dels Bandolers.

At a fork (**25min**) go right ('PARTIDA LA RAPOSA' is handwritten in red on a wall), heading directly towards Penya Severino and the Bernia Ridge. Walk through orange groves and pass a (probably dry) RESERVOIR on the right just before a

81

turning to the left — your return route (**❷**; **32min**). The road takes you past avocado groves and steeply down to the valley floor, where you turn sharp left on a track (**40min**). Cross the river bed about a minute later and begin your ascent. You'll be on this clear track for some time, so just ignore tracks off to the groves and back to the river bed and concentrate on enjoying the spectacular scenery. There are good views of Campana and Ponoch through the cleft formed by the Algar. The track zigzags up then levels out and runs parallel to the Algar Valley. At a junction, where there is a large ruined *finca* on the left (**1h20min**), go straight ahead and slightly downhill on a track — towards another house, beautifully sited on a little spur (**1h33min**). Some 400m/yds further on (at **❸**), a path goes right, past another large ruin, to the **Pas dels Bandolers**, if you would like a closer look.

The track now winds down past abandoned houses (diggings of wild boar are particularly evident here) to the floor of the **Algar (or Sacos) Valley** (**❹**; **1h49min**). The main walk turns right here (first put on long trousers). *(But Alternative walk 1 goes left and crosses the valley.)* You now follow the river bed all the way up the valley. *(**If you need to use the stepping stones at the first crossing point, it undoubtedly means that completing the walk will be very difficult. We suggest you do Alternative walk 1 instead.**)* The rocky track soon bends right, into the river bed, but you leave it after about three minutes, taking a narrow path which forks right and cuts off a bend in the river. Reach a CAIRN at the CONFLUENCE of the ALGAR AND BARRANC DEL CURT (**1h58min**). Continue on the (often over-grown) track which bears left up the narrower, cairned **Riu Algar (or Sacos)**, now in a little-frequented valley. We have seen wild boar here ... and a golden eagle soaring above Ferrer. After heavy rain you might get your feet wet if there is water in the river bed. At **2h08min** pass the first *finca* up on the left, with well-kept terraces and carob trees. You'll now have to walk up the bed itself for a while. The track passes through pines before reaching an open area, where the awesome peaks of Ferrer rise on your right (**2h28min**).

Cross the open area and follow a rough track as it bears left, following the bed of a new stream, the **Bancal Llarg**. As the valley begins to open out, the Carrascal de Parcent fills in the background. Ignore a track coming in from the right (**2h39min**) and carry on alongside a stream, climbing very steeply for a few minutes, past vegetable gardens on the right. When the track becomes an asphalt road, continue upwards, but turn off left on a track heading into the valley of the **Barranc** de Binarreal (**❺**; **2h48min**). When this track forks four or five minutes later, go up to the right and wind around the terraces. Pass below covered orchards and a RESERVOIR on the right. Reach the road again (**3h10min**) and turn left. After 450m/yds, just past a hotel with a tennis court on the right (**❻**; **3h18min**), take a concrete track off to the left and immediately fork left again on a surfaced track. Enjoy the views as it circles round the opposite side of the valley above orange groves. At about **3h27min** the track dips and asphalt gives way to dirt. Ignore tracks to the left and go up to the top of the rise (**3h32min**) which is on a right-hand bend. Pause here. You'll see two HUGE WATER TANKS ahead, beneath the gap in the hills that you'll soon go through. Immediately over the rise there are two tracks to the right. Take the first of these, going uphill and passing behind a house. It is very steep and passes under another house on the right.

Meet a concreted track at a junction (**3h40min**) and turn up left. *Nísperos* and olive trees grace the terraces to the left, and the huge rocky outcrop of Cabaix towers over you to the right as you pass below it. On rounding a bend (**3h50min**) the red-roofed 'NEXO' BUILDING comes into view, and you reach it at a narrow road (**❼**; **3h57min**). The main walk turns left, passes Nexo and heads towards the spectacular peaks of the Bernia Ridge. (*Alternative walk 2 turns right here, to return to Tàrbena.*)

After descending a little, the ridge disappears from view and the road bears right towards Campana and Aitana. The village of Tàrbena is laid out on slopes to the right. At **4h13min** you pass a concrete road leading right, to a few yellow houses with orange roofs. Some 130m/yds further on, take an asphalt track that goes up to the left and starts by running back above your previous route. There are almond groves to the left and the Bernia Ridge to the right. Ignore driveways to the left and soon descend between some houses, the Binarreal Valley stretching out deep on the left.

As the concreted track takes a sharp left hairpin bend (**4h22min**), go straight ahead on a rough track. Ignore a track going off left at an open patch and, as your track bends right, ignore two more tracks to the left (**4h25min**). Your view now stretches all the way along the Algar Valley to Campana and Ponoch. Pass a house on the left and continue winding downhill, past some ruins and towards the Pas dels Bandolers. A very steep track goes down to the right just before you go under ELECTRICITY CABLES (**4h45min**). In one minute you pass a storage shed on the left and in another minute reach an open junction where there's a small RUINED HOUSE (**❽**; **4h47min**).

(*Alternative walk 1 rejoins here, from the left, and Alternative walk 2 carries on downhill.*) Just *before* the house, take the track off right. Continue straight ahead along the edge of a field and join that very steep track you passed higher up as it winds — now less steeply — downwards. After passing through groves of avocados and oranges you descend steadily again for some time. Ignore a track off to the right (**5h03min**) and soon pass a *finca* on the right. Meet a narrow asphalt road and follow it past the small reservoir (**5h34min**) and back down your outward route to the CAR PARK at **Casa Federico** (❶; **6h**).

Looking across the valley to the Serra de Ferrer

Walk 13: VALLEYS OF THE SERRA DE AITANA

Distance: 10km/6.2mi; 2h25min
Grade: ● easy, apart from a steady climb of 300m/980ft during the first 45 minutes; all on good clear tracks (PR-CV 464, well signposted)
Equipment: see page 42
How to get there and return: ⛟ to Guadalest. Take the C755 west from the village and at the first roundabout go straight on. Almost immediately turn left up a narrow road signposted to El Trestellador restaurant and El Molí (Car tour 3 at 33km). Pass the restaurant after about 1km and 500m further on reach Font Molí, a small cluster of houses, with the old mill on the right. Turn right at the open area with room to park beside the wooden fence (38° 39.741'N, 0° 12.403'W). The *font* and picnic tables are just above you (*P*13a).

Short walk: Font Molí — Guadalest Valley overlook — Font Molí.
4km/2.5mi; 1h20min. ● Easy climb/descent of 180m/590ft. Equipment, access as main walk. Follow the main walk for 29min,

then turn right on a track (❹). It skirts to the left of cultivation, then cuts right through the cultivation to a *casita* (43min). From here the now-grassy track winds up to the right of the house, into another, partially-cultivated valley. Take a narrow path to the left of the cultivation. It becomes a little indistinct towards the end of the cultivation: keep a couple of terraces on your left and wind to the left of a dead tree, to reach the end of the valley (49min). Now climb out of the valley; you will see your path continuing ahead. At 52min you crest the ridge, and the whole of the Guadalest Valley lies before you. Notice, up to the left, the main walk track descending towards some rocks which mark the defile we call 'Chough Gully' — this is your goal. From the edge of the ridge, follow the path slightly left and head downhill, to wind around the top terrace. At 54min you join the main walk track at (❼): pick up the notes at the 2h-point, to return to Font Molí.

M uch of this walk is a pleasant stroll through a series of high-altitude valleys, offering a variety of interesting features. Birdwatchers in particular can look forward to some worthwhile sightings. Don't be put off by the climbing on the first stage. Just take your time and enjoy the surroundings.

Start out at **Font Molí** (❶): following the signs for the well-signposted and waymarked 'Sender de la Serra, PR-CV 464', walk up the road which passes to the left of two picnic benches. Ahead, on the left, is the *font* (*P*13a). It gives a steady trickle of water, but the main flow is directed down a *canaleta* into the village. Just before the *font*, take a rough path up the hill to the left. Meet a track (**3min**) and turn right, to start your steady climb to the base of Penya Mulero. At **6min** the track forks (❷). The main track goes straight ahead (*P*13b), but you must turn sharp right. On a bend to the left (**13min**), ignore two tracks off to the right. (The second of these, at (❸), is your return route.) On the few flat stretches, stop and admire the views: Aitana rising above you, the Guadalest Valley with its picturesque villages below you, and the coast at Altea in the distance.

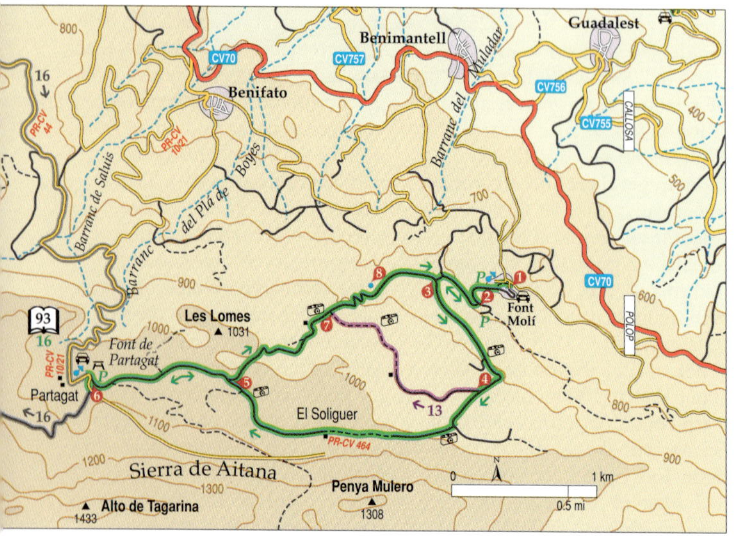

Ignore a farm track to the right (**23min**). In **28min** your track bears right, offering the first views of Penya Mulero — there is no mistaking this huge craggy rock with its sharp pinnacles. A minute later ignore a track going off to the right, down into a small valley (❹; **29min**). (*But turn right here for the Short walk*).

As your track bears right, heading below the cliffs of **Penya Mulero**, ignore a track off left to another valley and up to the main Aitana Ridge (**35min**). In autumn, patches of white and purple heather flourish alongside the usual herbs — but be sure to look up towards the crags. Not only might you have disturbed the noisy resident ravens, but you may be lucky enough to see a golden eagle. Whether stationary, perched on the top of one of the buttresses, or in flight, its size and colour make it unmistakable. Less startling, but worth a mention, are the black redstarts that flit around the bushes, and, in winter, the small flocks of rock bunting.

A saddle with a small hillock on the right and almond groves either side marks the end of the climb (**46min**). Take a last glance back at Penya Mulero and don't be surprised if you flush partridge along the next stretch. Entering another valley, you come upon EL SOLIGUER, a pretty *casita* not permanently lived in but still in use (**50min**). Descend gently through groves; after summer rains take care not to tread on the delicate saffron crocuses which push their way through the stony path. Benifató Castle comes into view at the top of a rise, precariously perched on top of a craggy outcrop in the northwest (**1h**).

At **1h03min** you reach a fork (**5**). You will later go down to the right, but for now go straight ahead. To your left are the antennas and domes of the military installation on top of Aitana; ahead lies another cultivated valley. Ignore tracks off into the groves; go past a chain between red gate posts (**1h18min**). The track leads down to **Partagat** (**1h23min**), a tiny valley below a spur of Aitana (see photograph above). Here there are a few houses, picnic benches and a *font* (**6**; **Font de Partagat**; *P*16), where you can refill your water bottles. *(Walk 16 passes through here.)*

Retrace your steps to the fork (**5**; **1h43min**) and turn left downhill. As you descend through this high valley listen for the raucous calls of chough and locate them much further down as they fly in and out from the high rocks. The track sweeps round an old ruined *casita* (**1h55min**) and continues downhill with views of Aixorta ahead. The Short walk rejoins from the right (**7**; **2h**) just before the track passes between high rocks on either side (we call this narrow defile 'Chough Gully'). Look out also for blue rock thrush and for the deep *nevera* (**8**; snow well) alongside the track on the left.

Continue until you rejoin the concreted section of your outward track (**2h14min**). Turn left and retrace your steps, either by descending on the rough path straight down to the *font* or by continuing along the track which leads you more gently to **Font Molí** (**1**; **2h25min**).

Approaching Partagat

Distance: 7km/4.3mi; 2h10min
Grade: ● moderate, with an ascent and corresponding descent of about 200m/650ft. A high-altitude walk along a fairly wide ridge (avoid windy days). Despite the lack of a path, navigation is only a problem in the event of mist or low cloud.
Equipment: see page 42; also compass/gps

How to get there and return: 🚗 At the 4.9km-point on the CV770 Sella to Port de Tudons road (the 23km-point on Car tour 4), turn right up a lane with PR stripes on a rock at the right. Park after 6.5km, at the end of the asphalt, by the Font Pouet Alemany (38° 37.835'N, 0° 14.870'W)

This walk offers splendid views and is high enough to blow away all the cobwebs. Short though it is, this is a must for those who enjoy ridge walks.

Begin the walk where the asphalt runs out at **Font Pouet Alemany** (**①**). A track runs straight ahead here, but take instead the sandy track bending sharp right (at the right-hand side of the *font*), going past a ruined *casita*. Ignore the track up left to the *casita*, but take the next one (about 20m/yds further on), heading for another house. Just before you reach it, two craggy hills appear in front of you. You are making for the saddle between them.

The track, rocky and in poor condition, goes past the HOUSE (**6min**) and then runs out at its upper terraces (**13min**). Make your own way left uphill to the SADDLE (**②**; **16min**). From here the mountain views are breathtaking — Aitana to the north and Campana behind El Realet (known locally as 'the Shark's Teeth') to the south. Stretching to the west is the Penya Sella Ridge with a sheer drop to the Sella Valley below. From here to the far end of the ridge there is no obvious path (so watch out for snakes!), but the walking is easy, and there is no danger of getting lost.

Turn right and climb to the FIRST SUMMIT on **Penya Sella** (**31min**). Continuing west, you'll see a couple of cairns. The second marks the second, HIGHEST PEAK (**③**; 1159m/3800ft). Now descend steeply over smooth rocks and then across the saddle, heading for a third 'peak'. This is in fact a rounded shoulder with twin summits, the first reached at **1h08min** and the second, across another shallow saddle, at **1h13min**. From here, you will see the ruined house shown opposite (**④**; CASA DE DALT), its

Casa de Dalt (1h38min into the walk)

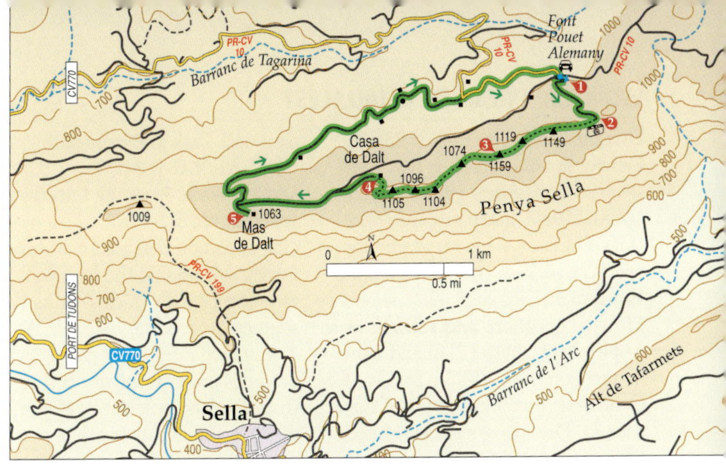

terracing stretching almost to the top of the ridge. Make your way down to the terraces and ruins.

Take the overgrown track going left from the side of the house and soon meet another track. Turn left and head west on a continuation of the ridge. Ahead you will see MAS DE DALT, a makeshift windsock indicating its use as a refuge by hang-gliders. As you approach this *finca* (**❺**; **1h35min**), a track joins you from below on the right. You will take this track, but first explore a bit — the house, a well, and the jumping-off spot for the hang-gliders taking the quick route down to Sella!

Return to the junction and go left downhill, a sharp descent. You pass an old *era* (threshing floor) and a few houses (**2h05min**). Meeting the asphalt road, turn right and walk back to the **Font Pouet Alemany** (**2h15min**).

Walk 15: PRESA DE GUADALEST

Distance: 10km/6.2mi; 2h25min
Grade: ● easy, with just two short steep sections (total ascent/descent 100m/330ft). The paths are good (much of the walk is on road), and well waymarked; you can't get lost.
Equipment: see page 42
How to get there and return: 🚗 to a point between the 2km and 3km markers on the CV755 just east of Guadalest (the 30km-point of Car tour 3). Drive down the tree-lined road, signposted 'Presa de Guadalest'. This takes you to the dam wall. Park in the car park (38° 40.697'N, 0° 11.541'W).

Shorter walk: Presa de Guadalest, south bank. 5km/3mi; 1h30min. ● Grade, equipment, access as above. Instead of crossing the dam wall at the start, take the track skirting the southern side of the reservoir. After 31min turn right on a track which descends quite steeply towards the river. Take the little path (44min) down to the pebbly beach at the side of the water (*P*15). Return the same way.

It is so unusual in this part of Spain to be able to walk close to water for any length of time that we felt this delightful walk should not be omitted, despite the fact that some of it is along the narrow service road around the reservoir. The reservoir is surrounded by mountains, and you will be able to appreciate their grandeur without the effort of climbing them.

Start the walk by crossing the DAM (❶). Aixorta is visible ahead (photo below) and the immense gorge carved out by the Guadalest River falls away on your right. The Serrella Ridge stretches along to the left and, if you look carefully at three trees at the end of the Aixorta Ridge, you will see Serrella Castle, well camouflaged amongst the rocks. Also to the left, Benimantell Castle (or El Castellet) perches precariously on top of a rocky outcrop (from further round the reservoir it looks even more startling). Directly behind you is Guadalest Castle.

At the end of the dam wall, follow the road left along the side of the water (yellow/white waymarks of the PR-CV 18 and 45). At times it rises above the high banks of the RESERVOIR before falling back down again. At the far end of the reservoir you will see the village of Beniardá, the antennas on top of Aitana and Benifató Castle — another astonishing feat of construction. The road sweeps round what could, in wetter times, be arms of the reservoir but the steep banks are now clad with pines or almond groves and, in more sheltered spots, with *nísperos* (medlars) and a few vines. Added to the calls of Sardinian warblers and whinchats are the calls of the gulls on the water — an unusual sound in this mountainous terrain.

As you join a road coming in from the right (PR-CV 18 signposted to Castell de Castells; **56min**), turn left and continue around the reservoir, sometimes in the open, sometimes through pines. Towards the END OF THE RESERVOIR (**1h15min**) you begin to hear the beautiful sound of running water deep in the valley below. The source of the sound becomes evident as you reach a bridge across the sparklingly clear **Guadalest River** (❷; **1h 25min**). Before crossing you might like to take a detour up the

Aixorta rises behind the Presa de Guadalest

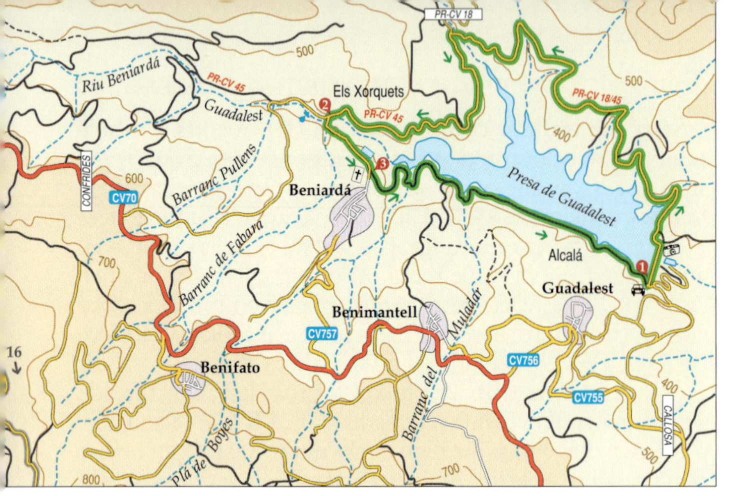

side of the river just for the pleasure of watching the water running between the reeds and cascading over the rocks, with two small waterfalls nearby.

After crossing the bridge the road sweeps round to the left and climbs quite sharply, passing Beniardá's municipal SWIMMING POOL (**1h33min**). About 100m/yds past the pool, turn off left down an ASPHALTED FORESTRY TRACK (**❸**). (The road bears right into **Beniardá** where refreshment is available.) The track heads towards the tail of the reservoir. When you reach water level (**1h40min**), continue on a path to the right, through some pines. A detour on a path going off to the left at this point takes you to the water's edge — a lovely spot for a break.

Return to the main track by the river. It crosses a little *barranc* coming down from Beniardá and passes through an area of trees and reeds. It then climbs, steeply again, to a wide track running along the SOUTHERN BANK OF THE RESERVOIR (**1h53min**). Take this track. Notice, on the right, a couple of minutes later, a section of an enclosed *canaleta*. Further on, the holes in the steep sandy banks of the reservoir are the nests of bee-eaters. These colourful, migratory birds are unmistakable, and you are quite likely to see them in spring or summer. It's a leisurely stroll back to the DAM (**❶**; **2h25min**).

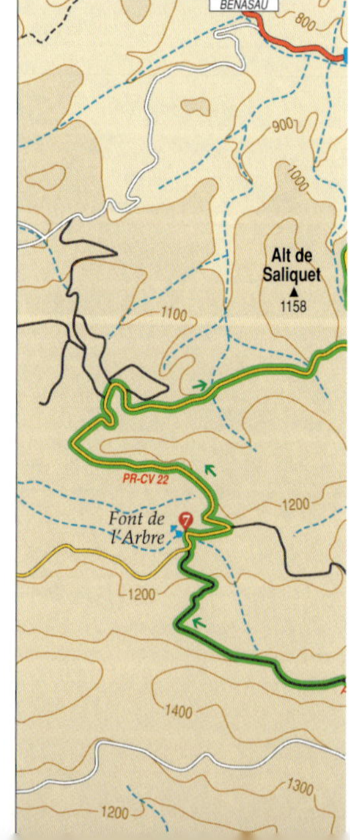

92

Walk 16: THE *FONT* CIRCUIT

See photo on page 87
Distance: 21km/13mi; 5h50min
Grade: ● strenuous, with ascents and corresponding descents of 600m/1970ft.
Equipment: see page 42
How to get there and return: 🚗 to Confrides (the 49km-point on Car tour 3). Park in the village (38° 41.071'N, 0° 16.259'W). No suitable bus.
Short walk: Three fonts. 7km/ 4.5mi; 2h06min (being an out-and-back walk, it could be shortened). ● Strenuous, with an ascent/descent of 300m/985ft. 🚗 to Font de Partagat (❺; the 40km-point on Car tour 3). Follow the main walk from the 2h06min-point to the 3h09min-point at **Font Forata** (❻) and return the same way.
Alternative walk: Benifató Castle. 9.5km/6mi; 3h35min. ● ⁝⁝ Access and grade as main walk, with an ascent/descent of 360m/1180ft. You must be sure-footed and have a head for heights. Trekking pole(s) useful. Follow the main walk to ❸

(1h18min), then turn right up the stony track towards the castle rock. Turn right at a junction (1h24min) and follow the main track as it gradually winds up closer to the castle. The walls become more obvious, as does the dragon's-back ridge on the southern side. You pass through an open area (1h47min) where the track bends sharp right. Cross a stretch of loose stones (1h57min) and turn up a narrow path through almond terraces. This takes you round the other side of the dragon's-back and steeply up to the CASTLE WALLS (❽; 2h13min). Take great care on this final, quite vertiginous climb. Explore the castle, then return to a fork just before the almond terraces (2h18min). Go right, along the foot of a scree slope. At a junction (2h24min) go steeply down to the right. When you meet a surfaced road (2h29min), turn left and follow it back to **Font Freda** (❷; 3h05min). Retrace your outward route back to Confrides (❶; 3h35min).

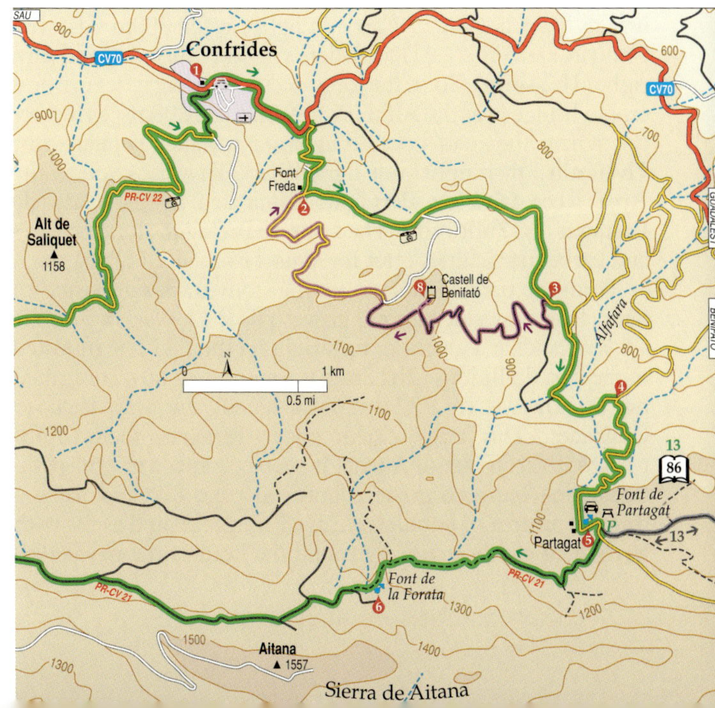

This magnificent walk is in three distinct parts: a stroll on country lanes with the serras as backdrop; a climb past several *fonts* on a path lined with wildflowers in late spring, coming within touching distance of the summit of Aitana; and a descent on a wild, isolated mountain road. For maximum enjoyment choose a calm day.

Start at the pension/bar EL PIRINEO (**1**) and walk back below **Confrides** and down the road in the direction of Benifató Castle. Pass a parking area and, a minute later (**13min**), turn right up a narrow road. This old road from Confrides to Benifató takes you to a junction at a house called 'FONT FREDA' (**2**; **31min**). Turn left, admire the Serrella ridge, and pass an attractive little house with a manège as the gradient lessens.

Approaching a CREST (**43min**) Benifató Castle comes into view. A few minutes later, at a junction on a right-hand bend, go straight ahead (left). The road descends for a while, then levels out, with the rugged peaks of the Bernia ridge in the distance and Aixorta to its left, closer to you. You pass a 30kph SIGN and a little later see Benifató village and Guadalest Castle to the left. Go under electricity cables and head toward the impressive buttresses of Partagat shown on page 86. There are several *casitas* on these slopes, and ahead are the radar domes atop Aitana.

As you contour between almond groves, notice a gravel track going back uphill to the right, heading straight for the Benifató Castle rock (**3**; **1h18min**). *(The Alternative walk turns up right here to Benifató Castle.)* Carry straight on for 300m/yds, to a HAIRPIN BEND TO THE LEFT, where you leave this road and turn right (**1h24min**). Soon the long ascent to Partagat begins. You cross a bridge over the **Alfafara** stream; then, 500m/yds further on, where the road goes straight on towards Benifató (**4**; **1h40min**), turn right (not signposted). This leads you to the **Area Recreativa de Partagat**, dominated by the **Casa de Partagat** (**5**; **2h06min**). The **Font de Partagat**, stone benches and barbeque facilities cater for almost every need (*P*16).

From the parking area go up the stony track signposted to Sella. Pass alongside almond groves *(Walk 13 comes in from the left here)* and, at a junction, turn right on the PR21, signposted to the Port de Tudons (**2h12min**). Your route is now confirmed by YELLOW/WHITE PR WAYMARKERS all the way back to Confrides. This track circles above Partagat, then climbs towards the cliff face of Aitana. It soon becomes a narrow path, zigzagging between gorse (photo on page 87) and passing through an area of boulders. Leave Partagat behind as the path levels then climbs gradually round the head of the next valley and up to where the domes on Aitana are visible again. Shortly after taking a left fork, you pass a reservoir and *font* (**2h48min**). The path resumes its ascent and, at a T-junction, the summit of Aitana is very close (**2h56min**).

Turn right on a track that undulates below the ridge. Pass a track off to the right and climb steeply once more, to reach **Font de la Forata**, in an open area with a signpost (**6**; **3h09min**). A path goes left up to the summit from here, but you continue straight on under Aitana's skirts and through pine woods, to the HIGHEST POINT OF THE WALK (sigh of relief!) at a junction (**3h18min**). Go straight ahead here, and also at the next junction a few minutes later. Before passing directly below the TV antenna, spot a *nevera* on the right.

Now begin the descent (**3h31min**) and admire the wonderful views into the valleys below. As the gradient steepens, take it slowly. In late spring the wildflowers here are splendid. You will soon see your next objective set among the terraces below. Zigzag down, taking the final obvious short cut to miss the last long bend and reach the **Font de l'Arbre** RECREATION AREA (**7**; **4h07min**). There are many picnic benches here set amongst the trees.

Continue past the *font* and up the main track, part dirt, part surfaced. It sweeps to the right below some houses and then back left to pass above them. Walk along the top of fruit terraces and a *casita* on the left (**4h27min**). Now in open country, the road turns sharply to the right, facing the Serrella ridge once more. Begin to descend, passing a complex of houses with extensive fruit groves (**4h45min**). Rise gradually past pines to a white *casita* at a crest (**4h57min**) and then begin the long, winding descent — perhaps accompanied by the wild calls of black chough. The stunning views change at each bend and are worth many pauses on the descent.

Benifató Castle comes into view once more (**5h23min**) just before a sharp left hairpin, then Confrides appears (**5h30min**). The road continues its steep descent through pine woods to a PR-signed junction in **Confrides** (**5h 48min**). Fork left here and sharp left at the next junction, to reach your starting point at EL PIRINEO (**1**; **5h50min**).

Walk 17: CAMI DE L'ESCALETA AND THE OLD ROAD: CIRCUIT FROM BOCAIRENT

See also photograph page 33
Distance: 12km/7.4mi; 3h26min
Grade: ● ‼ moderate ascents/descents of 300m/980ft; no navigation problems, but danger of vertigo on the return

Covetes dels Moros

Equipment: see page 42
How to get there and return: 🚗 to Bocairent (the 89km-point on Car tour 4). Follow blue signs to the Tourist Information Office and park in the old square (38° 46.040'N, 0° 36.612'W).

Short walk: Covetes dels Moros. 2km/1.2mi; 35min. ● Easy. Access and equipment as main walk. This stroll explores the network of 53 caves shown at the left. Hewn out of the cliff, they were once inhabited, probably by the Moors. While you can go directly there and back (signposted from the Tourist Office; 25min return), try this more pleasant, circular route. Follow the main walk to the bridge (6min). A couple of minutes later, *before* reaching the *lavadero*, take a paved path going steeply down to the left. Cross a stream and bear left. The path runs above a couple of caves and descends, to skirt the right bank of the stream all the way to the *covetes*. Metal steps take you up the vertical cliff to the only entrance. After your visit, return to the stream and turn right. Cross the stream just below its junction with a second stream, then strike uphill to the top of a rise. Ahead is the first Station of the Cross leading to the hilltop Sant Crist *ermita*. Make for this but, when you get there, turn left down a wide path. Cross an old bridge and follow a path to a cobbled road, where you turn left and climb back up to the main square (35min).

The Camí de l'Escaleta is the old mule trail which served the textile factories strung out along the Barranc de Ontinyent from Bocairent to Ontinyent. The waters of the *barranc* were used in the preparation of textiles, and mules carried finished bales to the towns. At times the *camí* is stony or well-packed earth, but there are some amazing sections cut from the solid rock — resembling bobsleigh runs! Pou Clar, a *font* with deep pools and picnic tables, is a picturesque spot for a break before returning along the spectacular old Ontinyent–Bocairent road.

Start out at the TOURIST OFFICE in **Bocairent** (**❶**). Walk up the hill, then down the medieval cobbled road to the restored BRIDGE over the *barranc* (**6min**). The road sweeps left, passing the village *lavadero* (**10min**) and a *font,* before coming to some houses and a CROSS, at a junction (**19min**). Take the middle road (**❷**), at the left of the cross. Walk to the left of some very modern houses (perhaps fenced off) on a rocky track.

Turn right when you meet another track and, at a WALK SIGNPOST (at your return route), turn left and go up a series of steps hewn from the rock. This is the start of the **Camí de l'Escaleta** (**❸**). Deeply pitted from the constant pounding of hooves, the trail takes you almost parallel to a track, then over the side of the hill, to another track. Cross this and locate your continuing trail, descending into the **Barranc de la Luna**.

After the first 'BOBSLEIGH RUN', the **Barranc de Ontinyent** comes in from the left and the first old mill comes into sight (**56min**). The trail bears left, down to the old building, and continues along the *barranc* to a second mill (**1h04min**), from where it widens to a track. High cliffs, pitted with caves, rise up out of the *barranc,* and terraces adorn the gentler slopes. The *barranc* has been dammed in places near the mills.

When the track forks, go left on a path to the third mill (**1h06min**). The fourth mill is the largest — about 100m/330ft long (**1h15min**). Not far beyond it, a disused *canaleta* winds past the fifth mill (**1h24min**). The trail goes under the *canaleta* and skirts the fence of a house (**1h31min**), before joining its access track. Turn left, pass a HYDROELECTRIC PLANT and reach the CV81 (**❹**), the main road between Bocairent and Ontinyent (**1h40min**). Turn right here but, if you want a break, **Pou Clar** lies 10 minutes to the left, just past the Fontaneta road.

The kilometre or so along the road verge is not very pleasant, but it's worth it to make this walk circular on the PR-CV 122 (or take the SL-CV 9 just to the right. It climbs steeply to the Alt de Castellar). At a WALK SIGNPOST (**❺**; **1h54min**), on the right, scramble up eroded steps and on to the continuation of the PR-CV 122 which climbs steeply before contouring round the hillsides, home to the uncommon black wheatear. Join a track and within just a few minutes, at the **Coll de la Dama** (❻; (**2h27min**), turn left on another track. This takes you up across open hills and eventually leads into another 'BOBSLEIGH RUN' (**2h43min**). From here just follow PR waymarks — all the way back to the WALK SIGNPOST of your outward route (❸; **3h04min**). From there return to the bridge and back up to the TOURIST OFFICE (**3h26min**).

Approching the first mill on the Camí de l'Escaleta

Walk 18: ALCOI • BARRANC DEL SINC • COLL SABATA • MONTCABRER • RACO LLOBET • MURO DE ALCOI

Distance: 20km/12.4mi; 5h40min
Grade: ● strenuous, with ascents of 770m/2520ft and descents of 870m/2850ft. Mostly on good tracks and paths; navigation is straightforward.
Equipment: see page 42; also gps/compass, long trousers, ample water
How to get there: 🚌 to the bus station in Alcoi. Then turn right along Avinguda Juan Gil Albert (the main road outside the station); it becomes Avinguda Alameyda. Just over a bridge (10min), you reach the Economy supermarket, where the walk begins. Or 🚗 to Alcoi (the 55km-point on Car tour 4 (page 31). From the Economy super-market (58km), use the *walking* notes on page 101, to park near the brickworks (38° 42.457'N, 0° 29.195'W).
To return: 🚌 from Muro to Alcoi
Short walk: Barranc del Sinc. 2km/1.2mi; 40min. ● Easy stroll. Access: 🚗 to/from Alcoi (as main walk above). Follow the main walk from the 25min-point to the 44min-point, then retrace your steps.
Alternative walk: Two of many options in the Serra de Mariola, where you can link up Walks 18-20, follow:
1 Alcoi — Coll Sabata — Cocentaina. 13km/8mi; 4h20min. ● Moderate-strenuous, with a climb of 440m/1440ft and a descent of 360m/1180ft. Equipment as main walk, less long trousers. Access as main walk; return by 🚌 from Cocentaina. Follow the main walk to **Coll Sabata** (❸; 2h). Take the PR-CV 37 path straight ahead, sign-posted 'TALECÓ DE DALT', soon passing this ruin. Keep left here, heading across a field towards a slope. The path undulates, then descends steeply to an unmade road, where you turn right. The road narrows to a path and joins another road (2h43min). Turn left here towards a quarry on the hillside

ahead. Meeting another road near the **Refugio de las Foietes**, turn left again. Then fork right almost at once for 'CASTELL, SANT CRISTÓFOL'. Cross the asphalted quarry road (2h58min) and head downhill on a track, watching for a 'CASTELL' signpost, indicating your ongoing path to the left. The path passes above a grand old *finca*, Mas de la Penya, then comes to a delightful spot directly under the *penya* itself — a massive cliff much used by Alcoi's rock-climbing fraternity (3h08min; *P*18c). The path continues to a narrow asphalt road (3h21min). Turn left uphill, past a chain barrier, to reach a crest overlooking Cocentaina Castle. From here take the path down to the left, to the castle *mirador* (3h34min). Now a concrete road leads you steeply down to **Sant Cristófol** (❼) — an extensive recreation area just above Cocentaina, with a bar-restaurant (3h55min; *P*18b). Continue down the road to a T-junction. Turn right and descend through the industrial area to a roundabout on the N340a with a work by the prolific sculptor Moisés Gil (born in Cocentaina). Turn right for a few metres, to an open area with seating (❽) — the bus stop for Alcoi. (But if you have time in hand, turn off the road *before* the round-about and see some of Cocentaina.)
2 Sant Cristófol — Montcabrer — Sant Cristófol. 17km/10.5mi; 5-6h. ● Strenuous, with overall ascents/descents of about 850m/2800ft. Access as for *P*18 (page 14). From Sant Cristófol (❼) follow the PR-CV 37 path (lined by wooden railings) northwest via three *fonts* and the **Mas de Llopis** (❾), then head south via **Montcabrer** (❹) and the GR7 to **Coll Sabata** (❸), then use the notes for Alternative walk 1 above to return to Sant Cristófol.

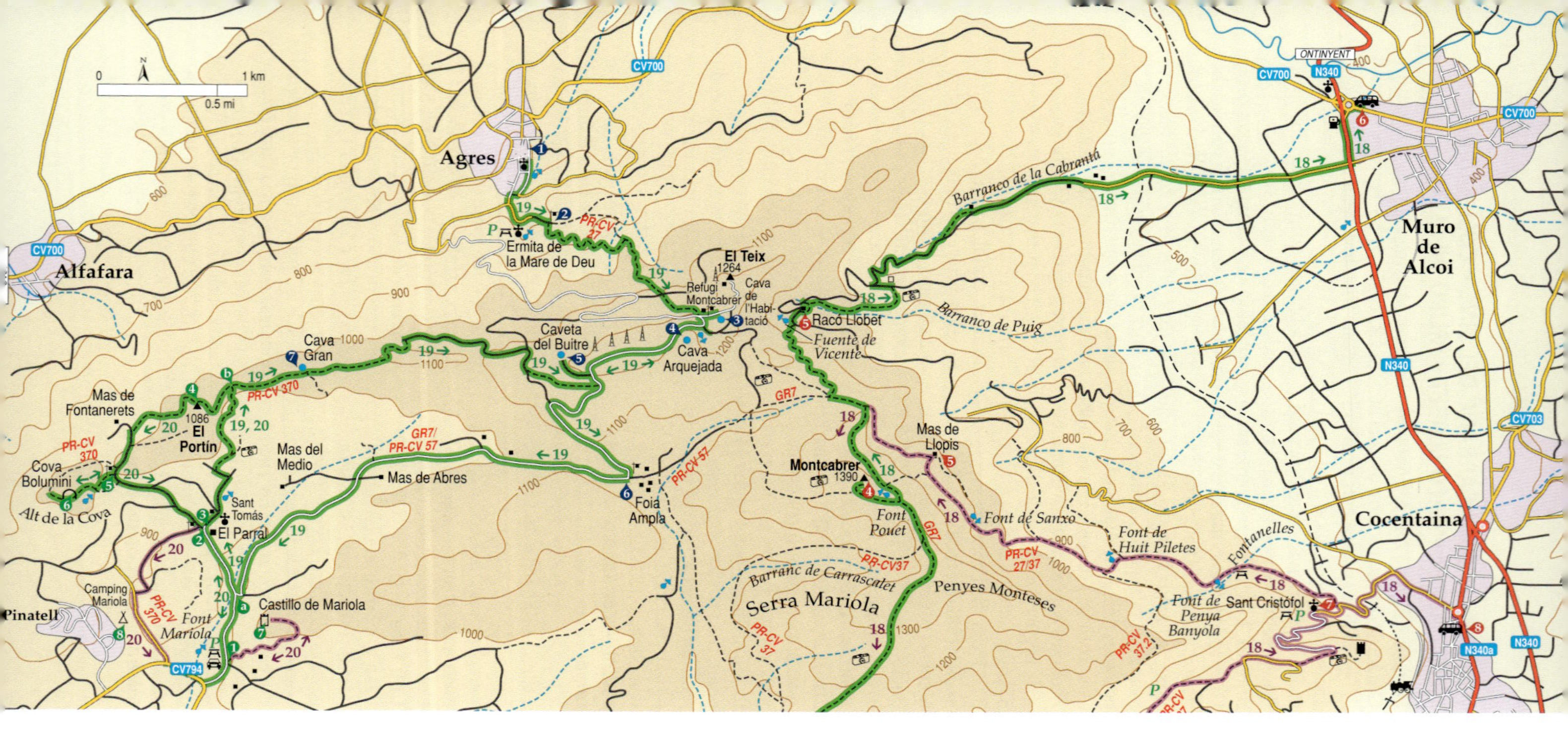

ONTINYENT
N340
N340a
CV700
CV700
CV703
CV794
Agres
Alfafara
Muro de Alcoi
Cocentaina
Pinatell
0   1 km
0.5 mi
N
Barranco de la Cabrantá
Barranco de Puig
Ermita de la Mare de Deu
PR-CV 27
El Teix
1264
Refugi Montcabrer
Cava de l'Habitació
Racó Llobet
Fuente de Vicente
Caveta del Buitre
Cava Arquejada
Cava Gran
Mas de Fontanerets
1086
El Portín
PR-CV 370
Mas del Medio
Mas de Abres
GR7/ PR-CV 57
PR-CV 57
GR7
Foia Ampla
Montcabrer
1390
Mas de Llopis
Font Pouet
Font de Sanxo
Font de Huit Piletes
Fontanelles
PR-CV 27/37
PR-CV 37
PR-CV37
Barranc de Carrascatet
Serra Mariola
Penyes Monteses
GR7
Cova Bolumini
Alt de la Cova
Sant Tomás
El Parral
PR-CV 370
Camping Mariola
Font Mariola
Castillo de Mariola
Font de Sant Cristófol
Penya Banyola
PR-CV 37.2
400
500
600
700
800
900
1000
1100
1200
1300
19, 20

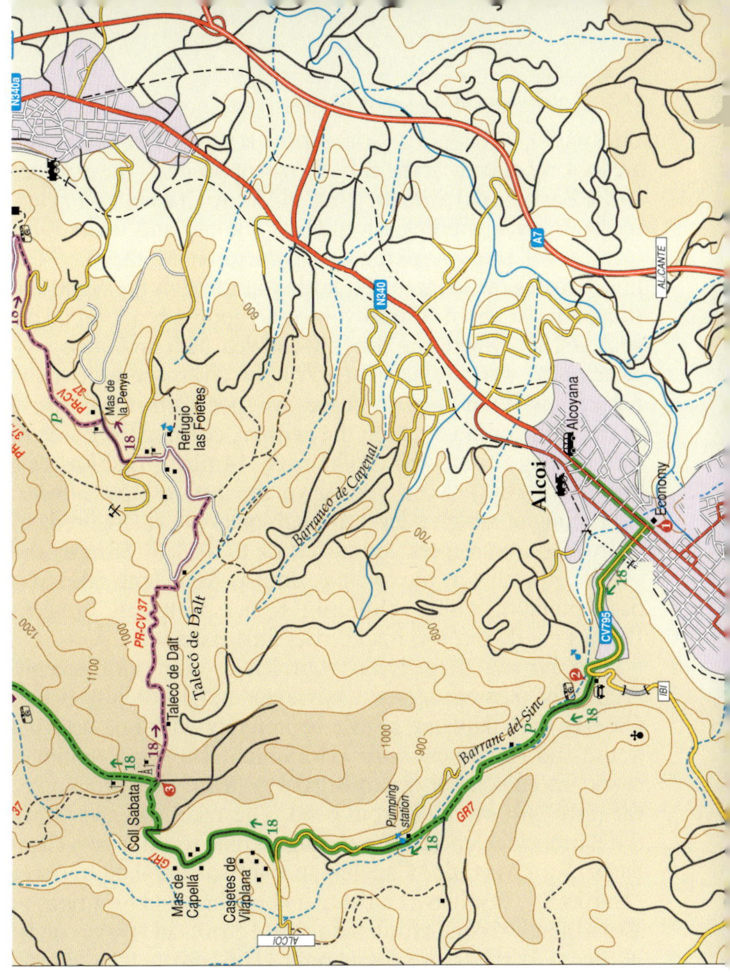

The Barranc del Sinc is a picturesque start to this walk, which takes you over Coll Sabata and across rocky ridges to the summit of Montcabrer (1390m/4560ft). It then descends into the cultivated valley of Racó Llobet and follows another *barranc* down into Muro. It is a delightful walk offering a variety of landscape and views.

Start out at the ECONOMY SUPERMARKET in **Alcoi** (❶). From its front door, cross Avinguda l'Alameda and go up CARRER ISAAC PERAL. This road leads directly uphill into CALLE LA SALLE and then CARRER BARRANC DEL SINC. Pass a *font* and the municipal SWIMMING POOL on the right, then an ELECTRICITY STATION on the left. Continue past the last row of houses to a BRICKWORKS (its chimney is visible ahead; ❷; **25min**). Those travelling by car should park near here, and deduct 25min from all times given below.

Take the track which heads right, on the bend, at the

brickworks (WALKERS' INFORMATION BOARD). From here you are looking directly at the cliffs shown opposite — the entrance to the **Barranc del Sinc** (or 'Cint' in Valencian dialect). You will see your track winding towards it. The red and white GR7 markers will take you all the way to the top of Montcabrer. The track crosses the *barranc* and leads you through the defile and to a path. At about **33min** you come upon a beautiful picnic spot (*P*18a), where the roughly-cobbled path and steps pass close to the watercourse. There will not always be water here, but even when dry it is an impressive spot. Cliffs tower above as the path continues along the *barranc*, crossing from side to side, passing a *casita* with a willow tree (**44min**). *(The Short walk turns back here.)* Now you leave the bed of the *barranc*, continuing at a higher level through pines which are home to short-toed treecreepers. Ignore a track to the left (**53min**) and continue parallel to the *barranc,* until a steep climb takes you past a pumping station (**1h05min**) to an asphalt road. Turn left. Being a cul-de-sac, this road carries little traffic.

The *barranc* deepens on your left as you climb steeply, eventually passing a LARGE STORAGE BUILDING just before **Casetes de Vilaplana**, a little community with one very old house and some new ones (**1h25min**). The road continues round into Alcoi, but you must take the track which goes up to the right, just on the hairpin bend. This takes you away from the Barranc del Sinc and up through a pine wood, past a chain barrier, to **Mas de Capellá** and its surrounding terraces (**1h40min**). Pass between the main buildings and turn right to ascend gently through fruit and almond groves and past a couple of sheds. As the track sweeps right (**1h51min**) take the way-marked path to the left and climb through a valley of pine trees to a clearing — **Coll Sabata** (❸; **2h**). Look out around here for Dartford warblers, which are resident on these upper slopes. A track and several paths leave from the col. *(Alternative walk 1 takes the path straight ahead here without approaching Montcabrer; Alternative walk 2 turns left on the descent from Montcabrer.)*

The main walk takes the path up to the left, past an enclosure containing an ANTENNA. *Ignore* the signposted PR-CV 37 path to the left (**2h08min**), and fork right uphill with the GR7 over pine-clad slopes where, in autumn, the heather is quite spectacular. Looking back once past the tree line (**2h20min**), you will see Alcoi spread out in the valley below, with the heavily wooded slopes and *ermita* of Font Roja across to the right. As the path approaches and crosses a shoulder, it becomes quite indistinct on the rocky terrain, especially in snow. However it is clearly marked with very large cairns and GR waymarks. The walking is easy, and the cairns lead you to a small crest (**2h49min**), where a deep *barranc* goes down left towards Font Mariola. We had to wade through knee-deep snow here one February!

From the crest, look for your continuing path making its way round towards the rocky outcrop of Penyes Monteses, which has a little pole on top. The path is clear for a while and gradually loses altitude. As it drops over the rocks to a lower level, it becomes indistinct for a short time. Keep about 20m/65ft below

The walker is a mere dot in the landscape, below the cliffs which flank the narrow entrance to the Barranc del Sinc (Picnic 18a).

the highest point of the ridge and look carefully for the GR7 markers. The path soon reappears and leads you round to the left of **Penyes Monteses** (**2h55min**). From there the path is almost level and takes you round to Montcabrer (you can see the craggy summit ahead). At the end of the open stretch (**3h03min**) the crags are directly ahead and, as the path winds round them to the right, you should leave it: take the little path up left to the SUMMIT of **Montcabrer** (**❹**; **3h13min**). On returning to the main path, turn left to a terrace directly under the end of the crags at **Font Pouet** (**3h25min**).

Continue on this path, descending at first gradually and then more steeply. Ignore a turn-off right to Mas de Llopis (**3h38min**; *Alternative walk 2 comes in here*) and reach a SADDLE (**3h44min**) at the top of the slopes above Muro. From here the GR7 goes left towards Font Mariola, but you should ignore this and turn right downhill on a path just a few metres/yards further on. You wind down quite steeply through prickly gorse, before contouring above cultivated terraces and getting your first glimpse of a house as you round a bend. The path circles above its terraces, then descends to a track (**4h**). Turn left, pass the dry **Fuente de Vicente**, and reach the house at **Racó Llobet** (**❺**; **4h04min**).

Walk to the right of the house on a narrow but clear path which winds right and then left, to a track. Turn right on the track but, almost immediately, turn right again, on a narrow path which runs above the broad terraces and leads to the **Barranc de Puig**. Follow the left bank of this beautiful *barranc* through thick vegetation, with Serrella dominating the view ahead, to a RUINED FARM (**4h 25min**). Turn left at the track here; about 100m/yds further on you meet the track coming down from Racó. Turn sharp right and continue downhill to a right-hand bend, just past a huge boulder (**4h35min**). Here take the path on the left. (Both track and path follow the **Barranc de la Cabrantá**, but the path is more pleasant.) Just after passing a *casita* (**4h43min**), rejoin the track as it comes in from the right.

At about **5h05min** you pass the first houses on the outskirts of **Muro**. Cross the RAILWAY and continue straight on to the main N340 (**5h33min**). Turn left to a PETROL STATION 200m/ yds away (adjacent bars, café, restaurant), then carefully cross the road to a ROUNDABOUT on the slip road into Muro. Turn right at the roundabout and catch your bus a few metres/ yards along on the left outside a shop, MURELEC ELECTRICIDAD (**❻**; **5h40min**; no sign, but the bus is used to picking up here). Back in **Alcoi**, use the notes at the start of the walk to return to your car, if you've left it at the brickworks (add 35min).

Walk 19: THE *CAVAS:* CIRCUIT FROM AGRES

See map pages 100-101; see also photo and notes on pages 6-7
Distance: 16km/10mi; 5h55min
Grade: ● strenuous, with ascents and corresponding descents of 820m/2700ft overall. The paths and tracks are good underfoot, except one short section along the ridge, where the path crosses rocks and is indistinct. Navigation is straight-forward (various PR and GR routes).
Equipment: see page 42; also compass/gps
How to get there and return: 🚙 to/from Agres (the 78km-point on Car tour 4). Park in the village, near the church (38° 46.796'N, 0° 30.946'W).
Short walks
1 The *cavas* from the Refugi Montcabrer. 10km/6.2mi; 3h55min. ● Moderate, with ascents and corresponding descents of about 250m/830ft overall. *Confident drivers and passengers* could drive up to the Refugi Montcabrer (near

❸) and start there: drive up the road towards the *ermita,* but then turn right opposite the third Station of the Cross. *Be warned!* This unmade road, although reasonably wide and well-surfaced, *is extremely steep with hairpins as sharp as hairpins can get and its sides are unprotected from treacherous drops.*
2 Agres — three *cavas* — Agres. 7.5km/4.7mi; 3h. ● Fairly stren-uous, with ascents/corresponding descents totalling 650m/2130ft. Access as above; equipment as page 42. This out and back hike takes in three of the four snow wells visited on the main walk. Follow the main walk to the 1h27min-point at **Caveta del Buitre** (❺; 1h32min), then return to the Refugi Montcabrer and retrace your steps all the way back to Agres.
Alternatives: This walk and Walks 18 and 20 interconnect, so a variety of alternative routes can easily be devised.

This walk takes you up pine-clad mountain slopes, down into a peaceful, sheltered valley and along a ridge with amazing views on either side. *And* there are buildings to explore. In addition to an *ermita* and a *refugio* (mountain hut), we pass four *cavas* (snow wells; see pages 6-7), probably all dating from the 17th century. Such wells were only built in exposed areas, where snowfall was virtually guaranteed — so, even on a sunny day, remember that it could be very windy and somewhat chilly up on this high serra.

Start out in **Agres** (❶): walk up the road to the left of the CHURCH (as you face it). Pass a *font* on the left and look for the Ermita de la Mare de Deu, your first objective, on the hill ahead. Just after a small PLAYGROUND on the outskirts of Agres (**4min**), climb stone steps on the right. At the top, join the road to the *ermita* at the SECOND STATION OF THE CROSS. Turn left uphill, pass the tortuous road up to the refuge, and reach the **Ermita de la Mare de Deu** (**11min**; *P*19). Take the narrow concrete road to the left, in front of the buildings, through the car park. Pass a *font* and take the track straight ahead, behind a CHAIN BARRIER.

The track climbs quite steeply, providing views down into the Agres valley. Close to the ruins of the old convent building, a SIGNPOST FOR THE PR-CV 27 directs you onto a path going right (**❷**; **15min**). The path runs straight ahead through pines, alongside a *barranc*. You cross this stream (**25min**) just before a path comes in on the left. There are many hunters' paths and short-cuts, but you will have no difficulty keeping to the clear, zigzagging, main path. As you progress uphill you will see two groups of antennas on the ridge ahead. You are making for the refuge which is between them.

When you meet a wide track (**57min**), cross over diagonally to the left, continuing uphill on the rocky PR-CV 27 footpath. Shortly after a pebbly stretch of path, the **Refugi Montcabrer** appears just above you (**1h10min**). This refuge (open and manned at weekends and holidays) was built in 1974 on the site of a ruined house, previously occupied by the workers and guardians of the wells. Walk about 100m/yds to the left on the

vehicle access road, to look at the **Cava de l'Habitació** (**❸**) — 7m/23ft in diameter and 10m/33ft deep, with a semicircular crypt roof (**1h15min**).

Return to the refuge and continue along the unmade road to **Cava Arquejada** (**❹**) which you can see ahead. It is probably the most beautiful and most visited *nevera* in Alicante.

The well itself is fashioned mainly from natural rock and has six upper openings and one lower tunnel opening. Take the road which continues behind this *cava*. In 10 minutes, as it turns left and starts to descend, take a track off to the right, which leads into the small depression housing **Caveta del Buitre** (**5**; **1h32min** 'Vulture's Well'; photo on page 7). This well has four access points, and its circular cupola is in excellent condition.

Return to the unmade road and head downwards. Within a minute or so notice a cairn on the right marking your narrow rocky return route. Continue down quite steeply, with views opening up over the whole Mariola valley and to Cava Gran over to the west. At a SIGNPOSTED JUNCTION at the gates of **Foia Ampla**, bend right (**6**; **1h53min**). In a few minutes, as you round a bend, look up to the top of the ridge ahead and to the right, to locate the circular stone building of the Cava Gran — your next port of call.

Continue along the the track past a modern house on the right, with a colourful WELL (**2h08min**). You will see an old *finca* set into the hillside ahead, below the crags of El Portín and the *cava* (**2h11min**). Continue on this main track as it rambles gently downhill, and eventually you will come to a major track crossing (**a**; **2h35min**). Walk 20 turns north here, to climb to the ridge above. You do the same, so turn right on the wide but rough track leading over the LOW BRIDGE, and use the notes on page 109 to follow Walk 20 from the 10min-point to the SADDLE at the 50min-point (**b**; **3h15min**).

Walk 20 turns left here, but you go right, along the top of the ridge. The path (PR-CV 370) may be somewhat indistinct in places, but you can't get lost if you keep to the TOP OF THE RIDGE, heading generally east. Come to **Cava Gran** (**7**; also

called Cava de Don Miguel; **3h27min**). Standing at 1060m/3475ft, its huge size and the thickness and solidity of its walls give it the appearance of a fortress. It is hexagonal, constructed on two levels and has three tunnels. Ruins of the workers' building are close by.

With your back to the main tunnel, go straight ahead, heading east along the ridge (over several small peaks). The terrain is rocky, and the path may be indistinct in places. There are various different routes over the rocks, but

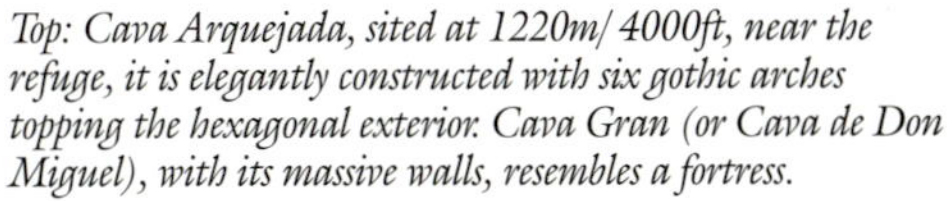

Top: Cava Arquejada, sited at 1220m/4000ft, near the refuge, it is elegantly constructed with six gothic arches topping the hexagonal exterior. Cava Gran (or Cava de Don Miguel), with its massive walls, resembles a fortress.

if you stay just below and on the right-hand (southern) side of the ridge, you will pick up the main path from time to time. At **4h01min** you come to a small SADDLE from where you have a good view into the valley below. The peak ahead is stepped with rectangular rocks, and the dense undergrowth on the south side is impassable. So climb the few metres/yards to the top of the saddle, and you will see a track coming up through the pine forest below on the northern side. Descend the few metres to the track and turn right, to round the 'stepped' peak and climb back to the TOP OF THE RIDGE (**4h15min**). Then leave the track just before it begins to descend, and take a path on the left; it continues east along the ridge.

Maintain altitude atop the ridge until you meet a wide track, the unmade road that was your outward route to Foia Ampla (**4h23min**). Turn up left here and follow your outward route back to the **Refugi Montcabrer (4h45min)**.

To return to Agres, retrace your outward path from below the refuge. Cross the wide track (**5h**) and zigzag downhill, ignoring tracks off to the right, until you reach the signposted junction (**❷; 5h38min**). Turn left and walk in front of the **Ermita de la Mare de Deu (5h44min)**. Take the road downhill as far as the SECOND STATION OF THE CROSS, where steps off to the right lead you back into **Agres (❶; 5h55min)**.

See map on pages 100-101 and photo below
Distance: 8km/5mi; 2h25min
Grade: ● moderate, with a gentle ascent of 220m/720ft to the main ridge at El Portín and corresponding descent. Paths are generally good, but sometimes overgrown in places. Part of the route is the yellow/white waymarked PR-CV 370.
Equipment: see page 42; also compass, long trousers
How to get there and return: 🚗 to Font Mariola (the 100km-point on Car tour 4). Park in the picnic/camping area (38° 44.759'N, 0° 32.454'W).
Short walks (both are easy; access as above; equipment as page 42)
1 Font Mariola circuit. ●
2.8km/1.7mi; 50min. Follow the main walk to the turn off just before

the *ermita* (❷; 19min). Turn left, and immediately left again, to walk along the edge of the pine wood and the ploughed field to the campsite (❽) visible ahead. Turn left on the asphalt road, and follow it back to **Font Mariola** (red and white GR7 waymarks; yellow/white PR-CV 370 waymarks).
2 Mariola Castle. ● 1.6km/1mi; 50min. From the picnic benches at Font Mariola you can see the Moorish castle atop the heavily wooded hill. Walk up the track (a post on the left is marked with red paint), into the pines. The track becomes a path, for a while following the boundary fence of a *finca* down to the right. After a few minutes it bears left up the hill and leads you to the ruins of the castle (❼). Return the same way.

Τhis delightful walk leads you through the fertile, well-wooded Mariola valley and up onto a sheer ridge overlooking the valley of Agres. You'll clamber up onto the

crags at the top of the ridge and walk through some prickly gorse (don't forget the long trousers!) to the site of an early Iberian settlement. Just over the rocky shelf, you explore a massive cave near the sheer cliff face, before descending back into the valley. Font Mariola is an idyllic place to relax and picnic (*P*20) — as long as it is during the week and out of season! You could easily combine this walk with Short walk 2 up to the castle.

The walk starts at the PICNIC BENCHES by **Font Mariola** (❶). Mariola Castle is perched on the knoll on the right, and your track runs below it, heading up the valley through mature pine woods. At a crossroads (**10min**)

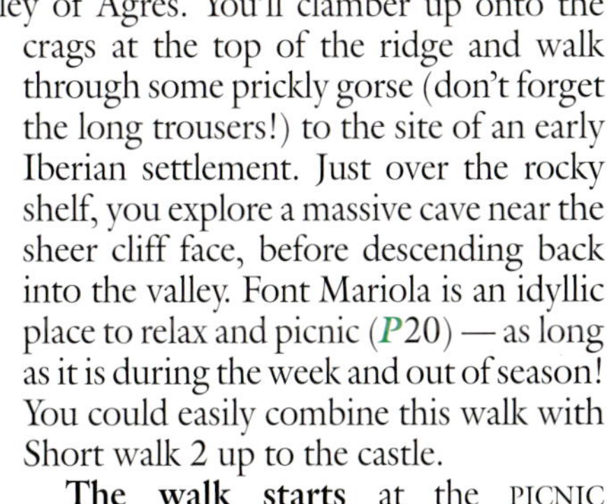

Opposite: the Mas de Fontanerets from El Portín, with the Agres valley in the background

turn onto a wide but rough track going left over a LOW BRIDGE (ⓐ). The main track going straight ahead (leading to Foia Ampla) is the route used by Walk 19, which joins you at this point. At **19min** a track coming in from the left is your return route (❷). *(Short walk 1 turns left here.)* Continue towards some buildings at **El Parral** (❸). On the right is **Masia el Parral,** ahead is the **Ermita de Sant Tomás** and to the left is a large red brick building.

Masia el Parral, once a magnificent *finca*, is now a beautifully restored rural hotel, and the surrounding land is private. However, you can ignore the *'No walkers'* sign attached to the building — it is there to prevent people wandering around the hotel grounds, and 'proper walkers' are welcome. But please respect the privacy of the hotel guests and keep to the main track. Do not be tempted to peer in the windows or wander around the guest facilities, including the swimming pool area and the horse paddock.

Turn left to pass the red-brick building and then follow the track as it bends right, passing a restored WELL. A few minutes later, just before a right-hand bend with a fenced-in stone hut and lots of standing water, turn left up a rough, muddy track. Look out on the right after about 40 metres for a cairn marking a narrow path. Turn right and follow this slightly overgrown but clear path, to reach a FENCE. The path follows the fence for a few minutes, before forking left and rising about 10m/yds across a loose and rocky surface to a LOW CREST (**34min**).

This is a good spot to take your bearings. To the right (east) is Mas de Abres, with Montcabrer rising behind it. The ridge with the *cavas* (Walk 19) stretches east to north from Mas de Abres, and your next objective — the crags of El Portín — are just ahead of you to the northwest. Turn left on a narrow path which rises, then bears right to run under the crags.

In about 10 minutes you reach an open area below a *font*. You can see the crags up to the left, but you go straight on. The path is a little indistinct here, so take care. Bend left at a cairn and walk though low scrub, to meet a clearer path at a small SADDLE (ⓑ; **50min**) with the yellow/white waymarks of the PR-CV 370. *(Walk 19 leaves here, by heading right on the path running along the top of the ridge, to reach Cava Gran in 12 minutes.)* Turn left with the waymarked PR route here, climbing up towards the crags. The path leads under the highest rocks, on the southern side, before winding round to where a short scramble will take you to the SUMMIT of **El Portín** (❹; **59min**).

Now, should waymarks fail, locate, slightly to the south of west, Alt de la Cova, a terraced hill which is the site of an Iberian settlement. It is your next objective. Also locate Mariola Castle to the south. Walk about 20m/yds towards a point between those two landmarks and, below, locate a rather isolated large rock that has a cairn on top. Make for this rock, to join a narrow path heading down in the direction of Alt de la Cova. The path runs along the foot of the wooded slope and then descends, through sometimes prickly undergrowth, to a track (**1h10min**). To the right is the *finca* shown on page 108, **Mas de Fontanerets**, but you must turn left and follow the path to a SADDLE below Alt de la Cova (**⑤**; **1h18min**), where there is a SIGNPOST FOR THE PR-CV 370.

From here several different paths climb the short distance, through abandoned terraces, to the plateau; take your pick. The settlement on **Alt de la Cova** (**1h30min**) dates from the fourth to first centuries BC, and clear signs of it still remain. Local museums house many artefacts from the site, and the whole plateau is worth investigating. Evidence of past cultivation abounds, and the plateau is so strategically sited that it is easy to see why it was chosen as a site by these Bronze Age inhabitants. In the middle of the plateau there is a small depression, about 10m/30ft deep. The northern (right-hand) edge of this depression is edged with a rocky shelf. Near the far end of the shelf you will see a path going diagonally downhill to the east (everywhere else there is a sheer drop to the Agres valley below). This easy path, shielded from the drop by rocky plates, leads in a few minutes to the massive **Cova Bolumini** (**⑥**). This cave also formed an important part of the settlement.

The PR-CV 370 path does continue past the cave, under the cliff walls and above a sheer drop, back to the Fontanerets track. But rainfall in this area is relatively high, and the combination of damp rocks and slippery grass means that great care must be taken. The more cautious (including us!) will prefer to retrace their steps up to **Alt de la Cova** and return to the MAIN TRACK AT THE SADDLE (**⑤**; **1h50min**). Turn right and continue down towards Font Mariola.

The track descends above ploughed fields, with the commercial CAMPSITE (**⑧**; where there is a bar/restaurant) off to the right. The *ermita* and Masia el Parral look magnificent down in the valley to your left. The track descends between fields, returning you to the track of your outward route at (**②**). Turn right and enjoy a good view of Mariola Castle (**⑦**) as you walk past the camping areas, back to **Font Mariola** (**①**; **2h25min**).

Distance: 15km/9.3mi; 4h45min
Grade: ● moderate, with ascents and corresponding descents totalling 800m/2620ft; tracks are good, and navigation is no problem (almost all on the PR-CV 26, a short stretch on the GR7).
Equipment: see page 42; also warm clothing, compass/gps (in case of mist)
How to get there and return: 🚐 to/from Ibi. Alight in the town centre, at the stop on Avinguda Juan Carlos I, off the main CV806 road: this stop is after the traffic lights. (The stop for your return bus is just opposite.) From the stop walk back northeast towards the traffic lights for 30m/yds, then turn into Calle Ramon y Cajal. Take the first right off this street and walk uphill for five minutes on C/Doctor Marañón, to C/les Eres (the main street). The *ajuntament* (town hall, with flags outside), is 50m/yds to the left. Or 🚗: park at the *ajuntament* (town hall; the 125km-point on Car tour 4; (38° 37.598'N, 0° 34.364'W).
Short walk: Ibi — Cava Canyo — Ibi. 10km/6.2mi; 2h54min. ●

Moderate, with a climb and corresponding descent of 500m/1640ft. Equipment as page 42; access as above. Referring to the map and PR-CV 26 waymarking, follow the end of the main walk in reverse to **Masía del Canyo and Cava Canyo**; return the same way.
Alternative walk: Ibi — Casa Foiaderetes — Barranc de las Zorras — Ibi. 12km/7.4mi; 3h30min. ● Moderate climbs/descents of 550m/1800ft. Access/equipment as main walk (except compass/gps). Follow the main walk to **Casa Foiaderetes** (❸; 59min), then take the track to the right. It winds down past terracing, lusciously green in spring, to a *finca* near the **Barranc de las Zorras** (Vixens' Gully; 1h15min). As the track begins to climb again, it makes a sharp right-hand bend. Leave it here, on the obvious path straight ahead (1h20min). It follows the *barranc* to a four-way junction (ⓑ; 1h50min). Turn right and follow the main walk from the 3h08min-point back to Ibi.

I n the 1960s and 70s the area around Font Roja was scheduled for extensive development but, fortunately, these plans were abandoned through lack of finance. However, it was not until 1987 that environmentalists succeeded in having it declared a Parc Natural. The ecological importance of its mixed woodland and resulting ecosystem will become increasingly evident as you walk through the park. You will also pass several old *fincas* — *importa*nt in their time, but now abandoned. At the Font Roja complex (*P*21) you can rest and picnic in beautiful surroundings, before undertaking the ascent to Menejador. As you begin to feel a bit chilly or as your legs start flagging as you climb, console yourself with the thought that you are attaining a height just greater than that of Ben Nevis. The return route takes you past three of the park's *cavas* (snow wells), before descending back into Ibi on a delightful old mule trail.

   Start out in **Ibi** with your back to the *ajuntament* (❶): walk up the street opposite (Av Joaquín Vilanova). You are making

Font Roja (Picnic 21). This walk takes you through its mixed woodland. Above 900m/3000ft the holm (or evergreen) oak, with its dark green foliage, dominates, but the humid north-facing slopes also provide ideal conditions for other species — Valencian oak, ash, and maple. Lower down, the oaks share the land with pine, deciduous trees and shrubs whose leaves, throughout the autumn, provide colourful relief from the monotony of the evergreens. In the past, the yew tree was also present in great numbers, but today only about forty of this species remain.

for the hills you can see at the end of the street. On your left is the more easterly of Ibi's twin hills, this one crowned by the Ermita de Santa Lucia. Just past C/Pinto Murillo, notice some stone steps with sturdy railings on your right — your return route. *(The Short walk climbs up here.)*

Then, just as the road sweeps round to the left, you'll see a track ahead between two BRICK GATE-POSTS (❷; **10min**) and a WALKERS' INFORMATION BOARD for the PR-CV 26. At first take the detour path to the right of the track, then join the track which turns left to cross a small *barranc* and climb steeply up the far side. At the top, cross a bit of asphalt and continue straight ahead uphill, towards a SMALL WATER CONTROL BUILDING and three pines. The track passes to the right of the building and goes round the head of the *barranc*, taking you to the foot of a steep rocky slope. The path up over the rocks is a bit of a clamber, but it is clearly marked and not difficult. As you reach each yellow/white waymark, look for the next one above you, so as not to lose the route. On reaching the top of this section (**29min**), you come upon a lone pine tree and can see the continuing path going straight ahead.

The next section climbs less steeply and takes you through herbs and gorse. Take time to turn and look behind you where, from left to right, you will see Carrasqueta, Penya Roja and the

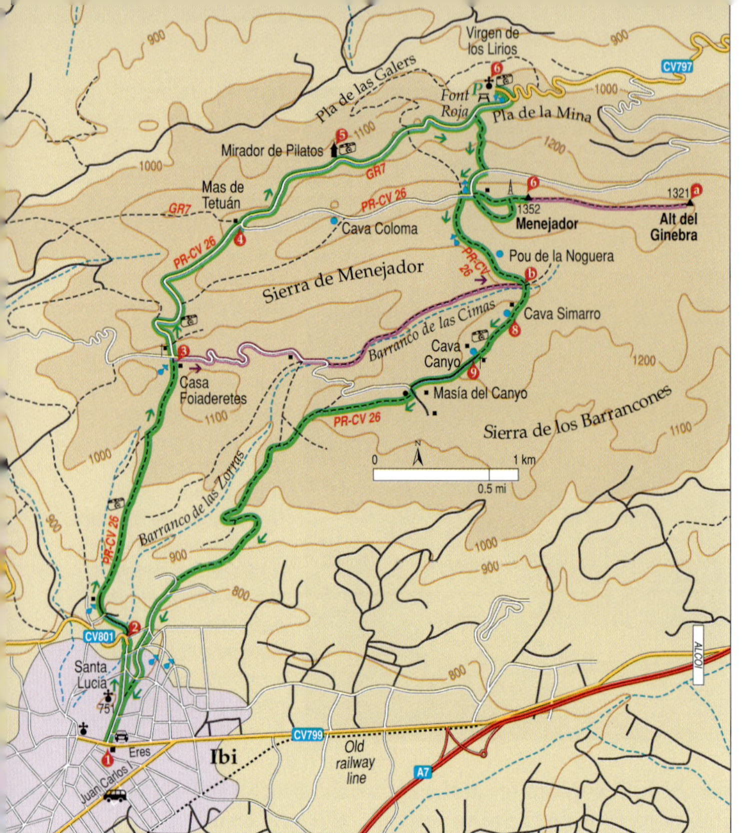

Serra de Maigmó (Walks 23-25), with the coast and *salinas* between them. At **45min** the path narrows and curls round the hillside, gradually gaining height. Ignore a path coming up to join yours from the *barranc* down on the left (**50min**). You pass some almond terraces just before reaching a good spot for a short break — **Casa Foiaderetes** (❸; **59min**). The house is in ruins, but its terraces are still tended and there is an attractive well nearby.

As you leave the house a track crosses your route. Keep straight ahead (*the Alternative walk turns right here*). Your track now rises steeply through a lovely area of mixed woodland, where you ignore a path to the right (**1h10min**) and pass the terraces of **Mas de Tetuán** and then the house itself (❹; **1h24min**). Yew trees still stand beside its old *era* (circular threshing area).

Walk in front of the house and, just beyond it, turn left at the junction, *leaving* the PR-CV 26 and picking up the red and white waymarks of the long-distance GR7 (a similar mark is visible on the stone wall in the photo on page 113). This is a park track, and will take you to Font Roja. Descend, quite steeply in places, past the **Mirador de Pilatos** on a rise to the left (**5**; **1h38min**) — an excellent place for a view down into the valley and up the heavily-wooded slopes of Menejador. Continue straight on at the junction at **Pla de las Galers** (**1h45min**) — so named because the *galer* (Valencian oak) is so abundant here. As you approach Font Roja, look well over to the left, where Montcabrer (Walk 18) rises imposingly. At **Pla de la Mina** (**1h54min**), the little path off to the right is your eventual route up to the summit of Menejador; but, for the moment, keep straight ahead: go down the steps through the picnic/barbecue area at the upper end of the **Font Roja** complex (**6**; **2h**; *P*21). The information centre is then just off to the left. Further down are the large **Santuario de la Virgen de los Lirios**, toilets, and another picnic/camping area with views to Alcoi and Montcabrer.

From here retrace your steps to Pla de la Mina and turn left up the stepped path (marked with a camera sign and yellow arrow) which climbs steeply to meet another park track. Turn right to a SADDLE (**2h30min**) just below the summit of Menejador. Here there is a junction of tracks and a large stone-clad WATER TANK. Do the round trip (little more than 10min): walk up the path, past the building and the antenna, to the SUMMIT of **Menejador** (**7**; 1352m/4435ft). (If you want to conquer another summit, a path leads eastwards to **Alt del Ginebra** (**a**), about 10min away.) On your return, take the track past the WATER TANK, but turn left immediately on the PR-CV 26 path (**2h43min**). It descends steeply past an old stone WELL (**2h53min**) and then levels out. You come to the first *cava* — **Pou de la Noguera**. This large open cavern is 12m/40ft deep and just as wide.

The continuing path undulates above the left bank of the **Barranc de las Zorras**, and you can see it going up the slopes on the opposite bank. Fork right (**3h06min**) and cross the *barranc*, where a path comes in from the right (**b**; **3h08min**). *(The Alternative walk rejoins here.)*

Go straight up the other side to **Cava Simarro** (**8**; **3h13min**). This 18th-century structure, the largest *cava* in this area, used to be the most beautiful, and has been partially restored. Above it are the ruins of a *casita*, but you should walk round the *cava* and up the slope, to a crest. From there you can see Ibi down in the valley, as well as the tiled roof in Arabian style of the well-preserved **Cava Canyo** (**9**), which you reach at **3h18min**. This is the smallest of the *cavas*; beside it are the ruins of the Casa Nevater ('Snowman's House').

From here the path widens to a rough track and heads

towards **Masía del Canyo**, a *finca* in a small cultivated valley. As you approach it, you join a track coming in from the right. Go past the house and its *era* (**3h28min**). You are now on a wide path, passing along the top of the terracing, and heading down towards Ibi. Ignore minor hunters' paths; keep to the clear main PR-CV 26 trail. You will realise from the still-visible hoof prints that this zigzag path, at times sculpted from the rock, is the old mule trail down to Ibi from the *cavas* and the *finca*. Descend past almond groves until you join an asphalt road on the outskirts of town (**4h20min**). Follow the road past a metal fence and between terraces. Keep straight on, then go down steps to join your outward route to the TOWN HALL in **Ibi** (❶; **4h45min**).

Walk 22: PENAGUILA CASTLE

See photo opposite
Distance: 6km/3.7mi; 1h53min
Grade: ● moderate, with a steep climb (230m/750ft) to the castle and then some scrambling
Equipment: see page 42
How to get there and return: 🚌 to/from Penàguila (the 41km-point on Car tour 4); park at the church (38° 40.759'N, 0° 21.544'W).

Short walks (● grade, equipment, access as above). Follow the main walk to the **crest** and back (2.5km/1.5mi; 1h08min) or to the **castle** and back (3km/1.9mi; 1h30min). You can shorten both walks even further by driving to El Coyao, the 37km-point on Car tour 4 (38° 40.356'N, 0° 21.516'W): pick up the main walk at the 25min-point.

This walk, largely on pleasant paths, is short but well worthwhile. Penàguila Castle, with its origins in the 8th century, was reputedly a stronghold of the great Moorish leader Al Azraq. There have been some restorations over the years, but little now remains of the ruins. However, standing at the base of its walls, one can appreciate the strategic importance of its position.

The walk starts in the MAIN CHURCH SQUARE in **Penàguila** (**❶**). Facing the church, leave the square to the right. Go through a second square diagonally to the right, then head left up the main street, CARRER VERGE DEL PATROCINI. When it bears right, go straight ahead up some WIDE, SHALLOW STONE STEPS. Cross the main Alcolecha road and take the concrete road going up the hill (still CARRER VERGE DEL PATROCINI). It climbs very steeply before crossing the Port de Tudons road (**5min**) and joining a narrow path about 10m/yds to the left running alongside a small olive grove. This pretty path, with all the appearances of an old Moorish trail, climbs in zigzags, crossing the road twice more. Behind you, to the east, there are magnificent views of Serrella and, on the cliffs below the castle, many caves have been formed by the erosion of the soft rock.

The path ends as it joins the road once more (**24min**). Turn right and, on the first bend, just past the KM15 MARKER, reach the gates of **El Coyao** (**❷**; **25min**). Take the little path that goes up to the right of these gates. Ignore paths off to the left and keep climbing, as you wind around the Penàguila side of this hill, **Cerro Castell**. The narrow path is eroded in places. At a CREST (**❸**; **34min**; *P22*) the ruins of the castle come into view, a large cross towering above them. From here the surrounding serras are spectacular, while Penàguila paints a pretty picture in the valley below. Now locate the indistinct path which descends to cross the rocks of the small SADDLE, below the ruins of an old tower. Take care as you pass the TOWER, and clamber up a

Opposite: You pass under this old aqueduct on the return to Penàguila.

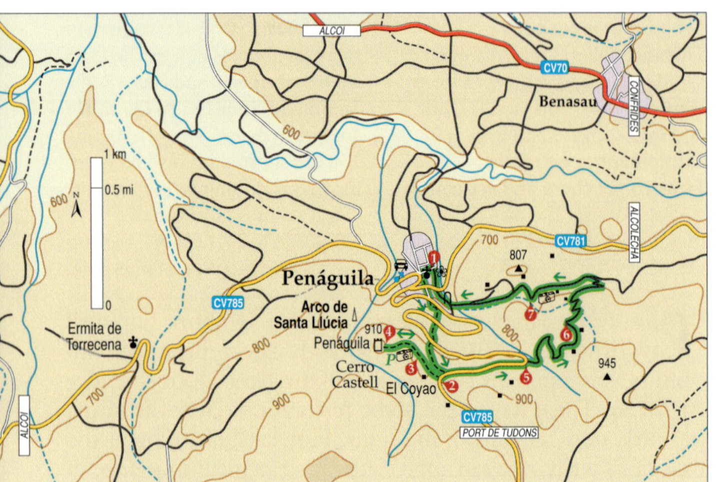

steep path to the rest of the RUINS OF **Penàguila Castle** (❹; **46min**). Explore as you wish — taking care by the steep drops to the south — and then retrace your steps to the CV785 at **El Coyao** (❷; **1h05min**).

From here continue on the road to the first hairpin bend to the left (❺; **1h15min**) and take the cart track straight ahead. After about 800m this track starts to climb, passing to the left of a house and aiming for another house on a saddle. Keep left here, but after 100m/yds be sure to turn sharp right (❻). You zigzag down past a third little ruin on the left. Across the valley you will soon see the village of Benasau, nestled under the end of the Serra de Serrella; below on your right, a track comes up from the village of Alcolecha. After a couple more hairpin bends turn left on this Alcolecha track and pass another *casita*.

Not far past a *barranc* crossing (❼), ignore the track on the right towards a house; go left up a small bank to join a rough, rocky track that heads steeply right downhill to Penàguila. It passes under the old AQUEDUCT shown on page 116 as it crosses a *barranc* (**1h46min**). It then crosses the Penàguila–Alcolecha road and continues through the **Jardí de Sants** (a 'historic garden') and leads to some steps on the left. These take you up into **Penàguila**. Turn left up a narrow street and reach the CHURCH SQUARE on the right (❶; **1h53min**).

Walk 23: LA CARRASQUETA: PORT DE LA CARRASQUETA • POU DEL SURDO • MAS DE LA COVA • PORT DE LA CARRASQUETA

Distance: 14km/8.7mi; 3h55min
Grade: ● easy-moderate; ascents/descents of 280m/920ft on good tracks and paths; some PR waymarking; navigation easy
Equipment: see page 42, Dog Dazer (see page 43)
How to get there and return: 🚗 to the Port de la Carrasqueta on the CV800 (the 144km-point on Car tour 4; 38° 36.283'N, 0° 29.158'W)
Short walk: Pou del Surdo. 2.8km/1.7mi; 45min. ● Easy ascent/descent of 75m/250ft; equipment as page 42, access as above. Follow the main walk to (❸) and restrace steps.

With the starting point at 1024m/3360ft, this walk offers splendid panoramic views for a minimum of effort. The variety of terrain, from rugged hilltops to gentle cultivated valleys, and the wealth of interesting features to be seen en route, ensure enjoyment all the way. Several properties in this area have dogs, some loose. Take a Dog Dazer if that worries you.

Start out at the **Port de la Carrasqueta** (❶). Follow the access road signposted to the hotel 'POU DE LA NEU' (also the yellow/white waymarked PR-CV 270) until it forks (❷; **10min**), then go right on the signposted PR track, which quickly reduces to a path. From here you have a fantastic view down into the Xixona valley to the right. Walk through low, aromatic vegetation and pass a couple of large cairns, one with an old IRON CROSS on it. Follow the path to the HOTEL and the **Pou del Surdo**, an old snow well at 1100m/3600ft (❸; **23min**; *P*23a). This well-preserved cylindrical *pou* (fenced off for safety reasons) is over 11m/36ft in diameter and roughly as deep. An iron ladder runs down the inside wall, and there is a mechanism for drawing up water.

From here a wide track will take you to some TV ANTENNAS (**28min**) and open up views to the left over the heavily cultivated valley, with La Sarga at the far end. Follow the track as it passes the antennas and undulates, gradually gaining height. In this area you might disturb partridge, and you will surely see and hear the thekla larks. Ignore side tracks and climb to a JUNCTION (**45min**). Take the track off left, up an embankment, and continue to gain height. We have seen golden eagles soaring over the valleys to the right. At the end of the ridge, a few metres/yards up to the right of the path, is the highest point on this branch of the **Carrasqueta Ridge** (❹; **1h03min**). It is only a minor peak (1224m/4015ft), but on top there is a cairn and a clump of Valencian oak trees. Surrounding views are impressive: the high peaks of Aitana with its antennas and Campana with its notch to the east; Cabeço d'Or to the southeast; Montcabrer, Alcoi and Cocentaina Castle (Walk 18) to the north.

From here *either* continue on the same track or follow the PR-CV 232 path ahead. Both rejoin at the SADDLE at the end of the ridge (**1h19min**) from where you climb past the head of a *barranc* on the left. When the PR-CV 232 heads off to the right, keep left to join a parallel track you can see about 100m/yds to the north (**❺; 1h28min**). Head left on this track, descending a spur, with *barrancs* on both sides. Ignoring side tracks, descend gradually through Valencian oaks, high above the Sarga valley. As you emerge from the trees (**1h56min**), there is an open field to the left and a track going to the right.

Fork slightly *left,* passing **Mas Plans de Baix**, a farm over to the right. Wind round the edge of its fields to a fork (**2h03min**), where you turn right on a path through pines. Descend to the fields at the far side of the farm and turn left on a wide track (**2h06min**). Caves over on the rocky hillside to the right (**2h14min**) house prehistoric paintings. On the left are the twin horns of the Carrasqueta Ridge. Reach an asphalt road at **Mas de la Cova** (**❻; 2h20min**); the house is now uninhabited, but its terraces are still well cultivated. This is a good spot for a break (*P*23b) and you can walk up to the caves.

Then walk down the road, cross the stream bed, and climb the road straight ahead. The road skirts to the left of the tiny village of **La Sarga** (**❼; 2h30min**). As you leave the houses behind, fork right on a dirt road. Then fork left (**2h36min**) on a track; at first it runs parallel to the track you just left, then it bends left between fields and through pines, up to a house (**2h46min**). Take the narrow path to the right of the house and continue past a small *casita* and a *lavadero,* up to a *font* in an OPEN PICNIC AREA (**❽**) amongst some trees. Join the track behind the *font* and turn right. Pass **Mas Els Pouets** (**2h53min**) on the right, a farm with its own pretty chapel and attractive surroundings.

Continue straight on to **La Lloma**, a collection of attractively restored buildings. Go round past the front of the buildings (to the left) and climb a track, past a storage shed and through pines, to a three-way fork. Take the left-hand path and continue above the terraces to a T-junction (**3h09min**), where Mas del Fondo is signposted to the left. Turn right here, then go left immediately on an old trail. As you pass under ELECTRICITY CABLES, cross a farm track and climb through trees. Go right at a fork (**3h15min**) and walk through some green gates, to the CV800 (**3h20min**).

Cross the road diagonally to the right and go up the track past the fairly extensive, but ruined, **Mas de Rovirá** (**❾**). The track winds up around terraces before settling in a direction

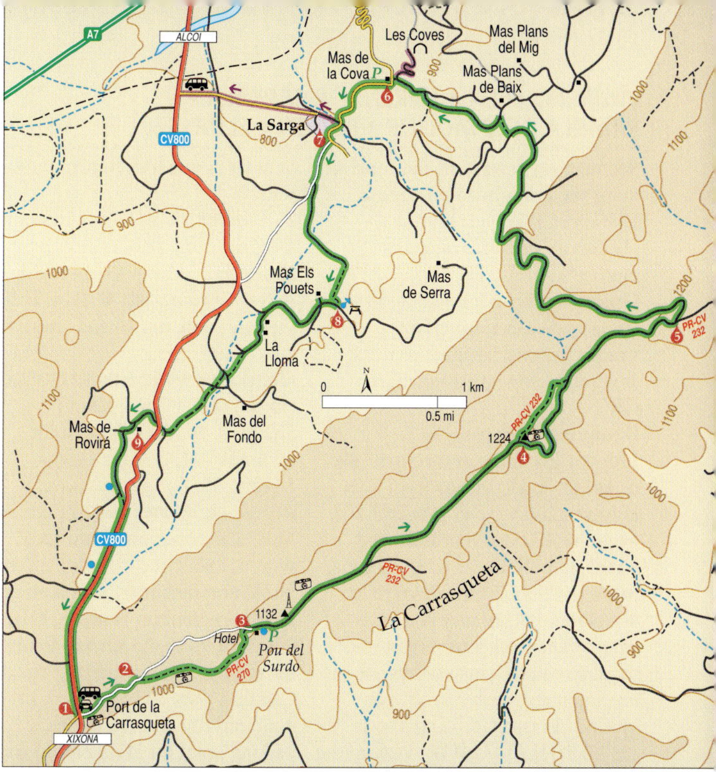

Pou del Surdo (Picnic 23a)

parallel to the road. It descends to road level at a semi-cylindrical *pou*, still used as a well. A track continues past the *pou* but, when it sweeps right, you must head straight ahead across the open ground that borders the road.

When a metal fence forces you down to the roadside, cross the road if you wish and continue for about 300m/yds, past another, enclosed *pou* on the right and back to the **Port de la Carrasqueta** (❶; **3h55min**).

Walk 24: ELDA • L'ARENAL • CAPRALA • RAMBLA DELS MOLINS • PETRER • ELDA

See map on reverse of the touring map; see also photo on page 2
Distance: 18km/11.2mi; 5h (15.5km/9.6mi; 4h10min for motorists)
Grade: ● easy but long. Good tracks and lanes throughout; straightforward navigation (much along the red/white waymarked GR7)
Equipment: see page 42
How to get there and return: 🚐 or 🚆 from Alicante to/from Elda railway station. By 🚗 take Exit 201 from the A31 north of Elda (the 46km-point in Car tour 5). Coming to a roundabout, turn sharp right, doubling back the way you have come, then quickly turn right under the slip road (see map on reverse of touring map). Park on the open ground close to GR7 fingerposts (38° 29.911'N, 0° 47.241'W). Pick up the walk at (❷).
Short walks (both are easy; equipment as above)
1 Rambla dels Molins. 1.6km/1mi; 35min. 🚗 Drive from Petrer or Elda to Restaurante Molino la Roja (❻; the 94km-point on Car tour 5; 38° 30.153'N, 0° 44.173'W). ● Easy. Follow the main walk down the *rambla* to the picnic spot (*P*24) —

or as far as you like. Return the same way.
2 L'Arenal. 6km/3.7mi; 1h56min for those using public transport; 2km/1.2mi; 36min for motorists. Access as main walk. ● Easy. Follow the main walk to (❸) and return the same way.
Alternative walk: Elda to Castalla via the GR7. 19km/11.8mi; 5h20min. ● Moderate (ascent 600m/1970ft; descent 440m/1440ft). Equipment as above. Access: 🚐 or 🚆 from Alicante to Elda railway station. From Elda station, follow the main walk to the 2h23min-point at ❺. This is also the 2h28min-point on Walk 25. Take the GR track up to the left and follow the red/white GR waymarks to Castalla (Walk 25 in reverse). In 4h50min you will reach the car parking point for Walk 25 and come to the bus stop in Castalla in 5h20min. *Note:* Just before **Mas de Angel**, a ruined hamlet above Castalla, you could take a very picturesque alternative route into Castalla by following Alternative walk 25-2 via the '**Forgotten** *Finca*' shown on page 15. This would add about 30 minutes to your total time.

This is a lengthy, but mainly flat walk between serras. Its two major points of interest are a huge inland sand dune and the Rambla dels Molins — a watercourse dotted with the ruins of many old mills.

The walk starts from the main exit of **Elda** STATION (❶): turn right into CALLE GALICIA. Go straight ahead on the main road, under the RAILWAY LINES. Cross the road immediately and locate some steps on the left going down into CALLE RÍO SEGURA. At the end of Calle Río Segura, scramble down the bank to the riverside and turn left along the canalised **Río Viñalopó** (**6min**). After going under a BRIDGE and across a rough section, you must make a detour round a *casita* and enclosure (**15min**). From here the water is channelled under-

*Castalla Castle
(Alternative walk)*

ground and giant reeds grow in the bed. When the path runs out (**31min**) climb up a couple of terraces to the left and make for a small building close to the *autovía*. This bears red and white GR7 waymarks, which you will follow for some time. From here the river sweeps left under a road bridge, but you must take a track going right. You will see THREE TUNNELS ahead: go through any of them, under the *autovía* and up to a narrow road (where motorists should park). Follow this to the left for 50m/yds, to a crossroads (❷; **40min**).

From the crossroads take the narrow waymarked road indicated by the GR7 fingerpost, 'CASAS DE CAPRALA/ CASTALLA'. Pass a long AQUEDUCT; then, when the road forks right at a WHITE WALL (**48min**), take the road straight ahead, and fork right a couple of minutes later (where the asphalt runs out). Pass between houses with market gardens, almond and olive groves, and come level with a sandy hill that locals claim to be the only inland sand dune in Europe — L'Arenal (❸; **58min**; *Short walk 2 turns back here*). There's an INFORMATION KIOSK here, open in the 'season' (out of season there is an INFORMATION BOARD nearby).

From L'Arenal a road initially takes the waymarked GR7 into the serras. Skirting a wide *barranc,* you pass between the **Serra del Cavall** on your right and **Cabezo del Pino** on your left. At a house (**1h11min**) ignore a track going up to the Serra del Cavall. At **1h23min** ignore another track to a collection of houses. You reach an open area with tracks leading down into quarries; then, from the top of a rise, the mountain valley around the hamlet of Caprala opens out to the left.

At a junction next to a ruined *finca* (❹; **1h34min**), take the track going down to the left. Cross the *barranc,* then resume the gentle climb into **Caprala** (**1h45min**), where the track becomes a narrow asphalt road. Follow it through the first part of the hamlet, which is mainly holiday homes, until another asphalt road goes sharp right, down towards a bridge just below you. Follow this down, cross the BRIDGE, then go straight ahead on another road, ignoring a turn to the right. You pass to the right of a VILLA (**1h58min**) where you will see the well shown on page 2 (although it has since been re-tiled). As the road finally leaves Caprala (**2h04min**), cross a *barranc*, pass a 'VIA PECUÁRIA' (pedestrian way) sign and, where the road sweeps left, go straight ahead on a track (another 'VIA PECUÁRIA' sign). This badly eroded track climbs through a narrow *barranc* for a few metres/yards. At the head of the *barranc*, you round a DAM WALL and join a broad track. Just after this (**2h09min**) ignore a track off right (waymarked PR-CV 144) to the Casa de L'Avaiol below the Serra del Cavall. Your (GR) track goes straight ahead, passing to the right of a large *finca* and cluster of houses (**Casas de Vilaplana**).

Continue straight ahead, ignoring side-tracks. But not far beyond the last building, at a junction (**2h23min**), ignore the PR143 track to the right. Follow the track in a bend to the left then, at the next fork, *leave* the GR by forking right (**❺**). *(Walk 25 comes in here, and the Alternative walk heads left uphill here with the GR, following Walk 25 in reverse.)* Continue on the yellow/ white waymarked PR-CV 143 as it bends to the right; ignore minor side-tracks. With pines on the left and groves on the right, you come to a crossing of tracks (**2h39min**). Go straight across on the PR143, now in open terrain with far-reaching views to Despeñador and the Serra del Frare in the east. As you round a right-hand bend, look left (southeast): beyond some deep and wide terraces, you can see the end of the Serra del Frare plunging dramatically into the Pantanet Gorge (Walk 25). Your track becomes a narrow asphalt road; it passes some houses in and meets another road coming in from the left behind you (**2h53min**).

Descend this quiet road through agricultural land. The Serra del Cavall is still on your right. When the main road goes right towards Petrer (**2h59min**), keep straight ahead. After passing a house on the left, the asphalt gives way to rough track. Ignore a track going left to a second house . In spring there are all sorts of wild flowers here, and the resident serins are particularly noisy. The track joins an asphalt road at RESTAURANTE MOLINA LA ROJA (**❻**; **3h14min**).

Walk a few paces past the restaurant, then descend the yellow/white waymarked trail into the **Rambla dels Molins**, a mainly-dry river bed (the waymark is on a road sign just *past* your path). It carries some water in winter and is liable to flash floods after wet weather — *take care!* Walk 25 continues from here up the *rambla*, but your route lies downstream to the right; so make your way into the river bed and enjoy a spectacular walk down to Petrer. The *rambla* is named after the water mills which used to grind the grain grown on surrounding terraces. Ruins of these mills remain alongside the *rambla*, and as you pick your way downstream — beside the watercourse or on a path along one of the banks — it is easy to imagine yourself in the past, leading your mules down this well-trodden route. As a path leads you left around the first of several (usually dry) waterfalls, don't stray up the track going left; take the path back down to the river bed. Cross it and continue along the opposite bank. The setting is spectacular as you walk under steep, sandy cliffs, with oleanders growing along the river bed (**3h30min**; *P*24).

Cross an asphalt road and continue along the watercourse. The geological formations are fascinating, as well as spectacular, with mainly sandstone on the northern, sunny side of the gorge, and a variety of much harder rocks on the southern side. A track enters from the right opposite a partially-restored MILL (**3h39min**). Behind it, other buildings are wedged into the hillside, some built into the cliff face, and a tunnel goes through the rock.

Another *rambla* comes in from the left where there are almond groves in the river bed (**3h44min**). From **3h53min** an asphalt road runs on the left parallel to your route. About five minutes after passing under some pipes, you enjoy an astonishing glimpse of Petrer Castle ahead. When the castle is in full view, reach an asphalt road (**4h08min**). Turn right and climb steeply uphill. Meet the PETRER-CATÍ ROAD (❼; **4h13min**), turn left and continue down to a MAJOR JUNCTION just before the *autovía* at **Petrer** (❽; **4h24min**).

If you parked by the FINGERPOSTS, turn right uphill here (signposted to Aguarrios) for 100m/yds, then take the minor road left. This goes along the eastern side of the *autovía* (don't go under it to the left) and leads back to your car (**4h50min**).

Those taking the bus or train should walk under the *autovía* and to the right of the CARREFOUR PETRER. At the roundabout, go straight ahead — all the way down CALLE DEL MAESTRO ALBENIZ. Follow this road as it bends right in front of the CEMETERY. Meet the main road and turn left; Aldi is on the right here. At a set of traffic lights by another large CEMETERY (❾), turn right downhill to a roundabout. Cross the road and take a minor asphalt road down towards the river and a SPORTS COMPLEX. You will see two bridges. Head left, cross the river on the SECOND BRIDGE, and clamber up the bank to CALLE RÍO SEGURA, ascending the steps at the end. In front of you is a railway bridge: turn left to the BUS STOP, or go under the bridge and turn left to **Elda** STATION (❶; **5h**).

See map on reverse of the touring map; see also photo on page 15
Distance: 31km/19.2mi; 8h50min (add 1h if travelling by bus)
Grade: ● very strenuous and long, with ascents and corresponding descents of 1045m/3430ft. Mainly on good tracks, with only one or two rough sections. Ideal for a balmy winter's day (make an early start!). From April to October, it will probably be too hot to attempt the full walk, so we have split it into three Alternative walks, each lasting about 4 hours.
Equipment: see page 42; also compass and plenty of water
How to get there and return: 🚗 from Alicante to/from Castalla (the 76km-point on Car tour 5). Follow the touring notes on page 37 to the fork at 78km and go right. Park neatly 350m further on, where a road goes right (38° 34.747'N, 0° 40.418'W). Or 🚐 to/from Castalla. Alight in Av Onil, at a bus shelter (ⓐ). Continue south along Onil for about five blocks, then turn right on Manuel de Falla. Turn right at the T-junction, take the first left on Dr Fleming then go left again on Av de Petrer, heading towards the crags of Despeñador. Keep straight on to a Y-fork with a cross in the middle, then go right; fork right again some 350m/yds further on. The walk starts here, 30min from the bus stop in Castalla.
Short walk: 'Forgotten Finca'. 6km/3.7mi; 1h40min. Access by 🚗 as above. ● Easy ascent/descent of 200m/650ft; equipment as page 42. Follow the main walk to the three-way junction (❷ ; 25min) Take the track furthest to the left; then, about 550m further on, turn right by a small building. Continue to the *finca* (ⓒ ; *P*25a). Return the same way.

Alternative walks
1   Castalla — Elda. 16.8km/ 10.4mi; 5h20min. ● Fairly strenuous (climb 440m/1440ft; descent 600m/1970ft). Equipment as page 42. 🚆 from Alicante to Castalla; return by 🚐 or 🚌 from Elda station. See notes above to walk from the bus shelter in Castalla (**A**) to the starting point (❶ ; 30min). Then follow the main walk to the 2h28min-point (❺), where you go straight ahead on the GR7. This is also waypoint ❻ on Walk 24. Use the map/gps tracks and waymarks on the ground to follow the GR7 from here to Elda station (Walk 24 in reverse).
2   Castalla — Mas de Angel — 'Forgotten Finca' — Castalla. 8km/ 5mi; 2h36min (add 1h if travelling by bus). ● Moderate (climb/descent 410m/1345ft); equipment, access as main walk. Follow the main walk to the junction just after Mas de Angel (❸ ; 1h05min). Turn left up this rocky track. Climb to a crest, then descend into a dip (ⓓ ; 1h25min). Turn left downhill here on another track, through thick pine woods. (Or first take a 2h return detour to the summit of Despeñador (❾): just continue along the ridge, enjoy the breathtaking views, and return to this point to continue.) Pick up the main walk notes at the 7h39min-point (ⓓ), to descend past ⓒ (the 'Forgotten *Finca*'), back to Castalla.
3   Frare Ridge and Pantanet Gorge. 9.8km/6mi; 4h05min. ● ‼ Fairly strenuous, with climbs/ descents of 500m/1640ft overall; you must be surefooted and have a head for heights. Equipment as main walk. 🚗 to/from Xorret de Catí (38° 31.156'N, 0° 40.606'W; the 86km-point on Car tour 5, page 38). Pick up the main walk at the

5h38min-point (**C**) and follow it to the 5h54min-point (**8**). Continue left (signposted to the Mirador de Catí), below sheer cliffs. From the *mirador* (25min) climb a steep narrow path up to the right (clear PR-CV 32 waymarks). Then clamber on all fours up through a rocky cleft to a crest (40min; photo overleaf). From here a path leads right to the highest point on the Frare Ridge (1211m/3970ft; 5min away) and on to Despeñador (a further 25min). But you should head *left*. Just after descending a little, the path comes close to the cliff edge, with fine views over El Cid and the Catí Valley (48min). Soon you see the complete ridge stretching out, with Pantanet Gorge at the far end. The narrow path goes all the way along the edge of the cliff, past several posts and giant cairns. The route is PR waymarked from the *opposite*

direction, so you will not notice the markers unless you look back. But you cannot get lost! The ridge is narrow, the drops are sheer, and you are going all the way to the gorge. As you approach the end of the ridge (2h18min), begin to descend over bedrock. After passing the last cairn, locate a PR waymark on the rock on the right (north) side of the ridge, and another on a tree (both facing downhill). With your back to the tree, facing due west, start descending, keeping to the bedrock. There are more waymarks on the descent and, as the bedrock finishes, you will also see waymarks below in the gorge. Reach the gorge at a walkers' signpost and a *canaleta* (**b**; 2h36min). This is the 4h09min-point on the main walk; pick up the notes and head left — through the gorge, past the Ermita de Catí (**7**) and back to Xorret de Catí (**C**).

This extra-long walk covers part of the long-distance GR7 . You follow wooded mountain tracks and then a rocky river bed through a deep gorge, to a spectacular dam. A country hotel provides a pleasant watering spot before you cross a high peak to return. Botanists will delight in the huge variety of wild flowers and plants to be seen in this area, particularly in spring.

Start out at the junction outside **Castalla** (**1**): follow the road on the right towards 'ERMITA DE CATÍ/ELDA GR7' (fingerpost) uphill through olive and almond groves, towards the serra. Go left at a Y-FORK (**4min**), cross a stream and pass **La Rambla**, an enclosure on your left harbouring a motley collection of deer, barbary sheep and peacocks. Pass the last of the obvious houses (**17min**), where the lane becomes a track and bends left. You have good views over the plain of Castalla to the left and soon pass two ruined houses, each one with an OLD LIMEKILN. The track sweeps round to the right at a THREE-WAY JUNCTION (**2**; **25min**). The track on the far left here is your return route *(and the route of the Short walk),* but you go right following the GR waymarks. Pass the chained track to an abandoned *finca* on the right (**30min**). Steep crags rise above. At **53min** come to a faded sign to Finca Fermosa, and a chain across the road. Walk behind the chain and continue to the top

of the serra. The ruins of a *finca*, **Mas de Angel**, are on the right (**1h**); the terraces are still cultivated. This whole plateau is known as **Fermosas**.

As you continue on the track note a WELL down in a field on the right. The TRACK off left just past this well (❸; **1h05min**) leads along the ridge of the Serra de Maigmó to Despeñador — your return route. *(Alternative walk 2 heads up left here.)* Continue through woodland across this high plateau, with the Serra de l'Arguenya on the right. All the buildings up here are abandoned, but the plateau is still heavily cultivated.

At a junction (**1h16min**) be sure to fork *left* — even if you see some old GR waymarks on the track to the right. Ten minutes later pass a track on the right which may also have old GR waymarks; ignore it. Ignore, too, all side-tracks as you begin to descend from the Fermosas plateau. The valley below opens out to the west, with views as far as the salt marshes beyond Elda, and to all the serras stretching out in the distance. At **2h06min** a short-cut path down to the right cuts off a bend, but the main track is easier walking.

A TRACK CROSSES yours as you reach more open terrain and the incline lessens (❹; **2h13min**). The prominent flat top and twin peaks of El Cid dominate the skyline to the south. You are now walking through land belonging to the *finca* **Costa o Novayal**, visible on your right. Ignore tracks to the left and right. Two small cylindrical stone constructions are visible in the fields on the left. You pass under ELECTRICITY CABLES by the second of these; a collection of buildings and a *finca* are ahead. After passing a chain barrier, but before reaching the first building, you come to a JUNCTION (**5**; **2h28min**). Turn left. (*Alternative walk 1 bears right here on the GR7, and Alternative walk 24 comes in here, en route to Castalla.*)

The next section of the walk is common to this walk and Walk 24; pick up the notes for Walk 24 at the 2h23min-point (page 124) and follow them to the RESTAURANTE MOLINO LA ROJA (**6**; **3h19min**). Below the restaurant is a river bed — **Rambla dels Molins**.

Walk 24 follows this downstream to Petrer, but you turn left, upstream, walking on the flat rocks of the river bed for a short while. The *rambla* does contain some water throughout the winter, and after heavy rain there can be flash floods — so be aware. When you reach an asphalt road (**3h29min**), turn right, up towards Catí. The road sweeps round to the left (**3h38min**); then, just before a 90° bend to the right, climb a track up right past **Casa de la Loma**, a small *finca*. Just before the house, above you on the left, there is a fine *era* (grain-milling slab) and a millstone.

The track, now little more than a path, continues up the hill alongside almond groves and meets the asphalt road again (**4h**). Cross the road and locate a path, slightly to the left, with PR waymarkings; it leads through a pine wood. (There is a wider track going downhill alongside these groves, but your path begins to the right of this track and slightly higher up.) This path leads you into the spectacular **Pantanet Gorge** which you saw from the Casas de Villaplana. Turn right and make your way over the rocks and up through the gorge, passing a SIGNPOSTED PATH coming down the rocks on your left, on the far side of a *canaleta* (**b**; **4h09min**). (*Alternative walk 3 comes down here.*) At the end of the gorge a huge DAM WALL towers above you (**4h16min**). It is an easy clamber up the rocks to the left, to join the continuation of the path; it takes you back to the asphalt road (**4h20min**).

This road continues left uphill to Catí, 3km away. But you must go right for about 300m/yds. Just opposite the entrance to CASA PANTANET, take the PR-CV 143 path to the left; it will take you up to the **Coll de Moros**. It's a steady climb up to this ridge, with lovely views of the craggy Serra del Frare to your left. Meet a track coming up from the valley on your right (**4h51min**) and follow it to the left. It continues the gentle climb, then levels out. Pass a signposted footpath coming in from the right, before reaching the **Ermita de Catí** (**7**; **5h18min**; *P*25b), a lovely spot for a break. From the *ermita*, there are wonderful views across to El Cid and the Serra de Maigmó to the south and east.

Leaving the *ermita* on the same track, you come to a junction: fork left downhill, passing a track off left (**5h29min**) to the CASA DE LA ADMINISTRACIÓN and a fine example of a *cava* nearby. Your track heads right and then turns right, joining a poorly surfaced asphalt road to a modern hotel with excellent facilities — XORRET DE CATÍ (●; **5h38min**).

From the hotel, take the asphalt road west towards Petrer, but after 100m/yds turn right towards the 'MIRADOR DE CATÍ', on a wide track with PR signposting. The crags of Despeñador tower above, as you climb steadily. Ignore side-tracks, including the one to Casa de la Coveta on the left. But when the track sweeps round to the left (signposted to the *mirador*), take the narrower track straight ahead (❽; PR signpost; **5h54min**). *(But go left for Alternative walk 3.)*

Fork left (**6h01min**) and, at a T-junction 200m/yds further on, turn left again on another track. This track curls round right and right again to an asphalt road, where you turn left. After about 100m/yds you will reach a crest, the **Coll del Portell** (**6h19min**), where there is a brick WATER DEPOSIT. Take the PR-signposted path up left alongside its fence; a steady climb brings you to the ridge (**6h34min**). Turn right to the SUMMIT of **Despeñador** (❾; **6h40min**). The views are among the most spectacular we have seen in all of our walks in Alicante, with about 30 serras being identifiable. It is absolutely breathtaking on a clear day.

Follow the clear track off the summit, initially going west and then northwest along the ridge. A track joins you from the right (from the Catí-Castalla road; **7h11min**). Ignore paths down into the valley on your left. When your track begins to drop sharply into a dip, in a small clearing (❿; **7h39min**), look for a narrower, eroded track going down to the right and take it. *(Alternative walk 2 comes in here from Mas de Angel.)* At at fork (**7h49min**) go left. About six minutes later take a track running obliquely left; it contours round some terraces and suddenly reveals the old but substantial *finca* (**8h**) shown on page 15. As it is so secluded and not named on any maps, we call it the 'FORGOTTEN *FINCA*' (●; *P*25a).

Just before the *finca* was a track off right, alongside terraces. Take it now. Rough and rocky, it becomes a path which descends alongside a *barranc*. It widens out again and, at a junction near a *casita*, joins another track. Just before joining this track, turn left on a path going up behind the *casita* (**8h20min**). The path soon becomes a track and meets your outward route at the THREE-WAY JUNCTION (**8h29min**). Turn right downhill, past the LIMEKILNS, to your starting point outside **Castalla** (**8h50min**).

Map on reverse of the touring map
Distance: 10.5km/6.5mi; 3h15min
Grade: ● moderate, with ascents and corresponding descents of about 500m/1650ft; navigation straightforward throughout (yellow/white waymarked PR-CV 155)
Equipment: see page 42
How to get there and return: 🚗 to Biar. From the 70km-point on Car tour 5 take the exit for Castalla and Biar. *Note the distance here.* Just over 4km from the CV80 watch for the gated entrance to a factory on the left, then a red-surfaced cycle track on the right. Take the next left turn, where there is a sign on the left prohibiting lorries over 3.5t) but *no other signposting.* Follow the one-way arrow and keep straight ahead over a roundabout, going uphill, to a T-junction. Turn left and drive uphill to where the asphalt ends at a forestry road. Park in the open space on the right (38° 37.168'N, 0° 45.725'W).

Short walks: The Biar Nature Association has established three botanical trails in the Serra del Frare; all start at the 10min-point in our walk (ⓐ). **1) Green trail:** ● short (2km) and primarily for schoolchildren, this runs west past the **Casa del Frare** (❼) and ends about 500m further on. **2) Blue trail:** ● 5km; this follows our walk, then heads northwest from the **Alto del Redondo** (❷), back to the **Casa del Frare** (❼) and the start. **3) Red trail:** ● 7km; this follows our walk, heads northwest past **Cova Roja** (❸), visits the SUMMIT (❺) and returns as our walk.
Longer walk: PR-CV 155 from La Mare de Déu. ● 15km/9.3mi; 4h30min. The PR-CV 155 'officially' starts at the Santuari de la Mare de Déu de Grácia, east of Biar (see map; 38° 37.788'N, 0° 45.077'W). You could follow it from there and back.

A major summit, a lovely old trail, and fantastic views all contribute to the magic of this walk. Located in one of the cooler parts of the region, the almond trees blossom later here than elsewhere, making this a perfect walk for a warm day in mid-March. There are several ways of shortening the walk, and the red trail mentioned above is our favourite. Many of the plants along the trails are labelled — among them the thyme, juniper, helichrysum, rock rose, kermes oak, and buckthorn which support the fauna of the Serra del Frare.

Start the walk at the PARKING PLACE (❶) by going up the forestry road and round a hairpin bend. The junction where a track comes down from the right (ⓐ; **10min**) marks the starting point for all the nature trails. You will return this way, but for now keep ahead on the track until the yellow/white-waymarked PR-CV 155 points you right, up to the top of **Alto del Redondo** (❷; **40min**), with its fine views. The blue trail heads northwest from here, but the PR and the red route leads you zigzagging down a beautiful old stone-laid mule trail, **El Comptador**.

Touching on the forestry track again, follow the waymarks to the right, to **Cova Roja** (❸). (The red-waymarked trail heads northwest from here, at first via a pebbly *barranc* and then beside it on a rocky path, to the Fonteta de Sant Joan and on to the summit of Frare.) The yellow/white PR155, our route, short-cuts the track, then rejoins it for another 2km, passing the **Font del Destallador** (**4**) about halfway along.

Just after a zigzag bend, follow the yellow and white way-marks up to the right, to gain the ridge path. From the SUMMIT and TRIG POINT on the **Serra del Frare** (**5**; 1042m/3420ft; **2h10min**) you enjoy fine views to the left across the heavily cultivated Biar Valley and to the right over the Sax Valley.

You meet the red path again here, heading directly back to the start. But first follow the PR down to the **Font de Sant Joan** (**6**; unfortunately dry and locked on our last visit). The route then rises northeast to a CREST, where you follow the track to the right, descending past some interesting old stone distance markers to a junction (**3h**). Here there is an antenna alongside the fairly extensive ruins of the **Casa del Frare** (**7**), and a good view down into Biar, overlooked by its prominent castle.

Take the right-hand track and reach the forestry road of your outward route, where you turn left and head back down to your PARKING PLACE (**1**; **3h15min**).

On the red-waymarked trail

BUS AND TRAIN TIMETABLES

Several bus companies operate in the area covered by this guide. There is also a narrow-gauge railway called TRAM running between Alicante and Dénia. All their websites are shown beside the relevant timetables below, but be warned: even when the websites are in English, they are *not* user-friendly. Note that there is far more coverage than stated here; if you will be relying on public transport, we **strongly recommend** visiting the nearest bus or train station for the latest timetables and information about all the routes they cover and possible passes for travel at a reduced rate. .

Albir–Benidorm (alicante.avanzagrupo.com/en); Bus No 10; daily; journey time 25min. *Recheck times: website down at press date!*
Departs Albir every half hour at 25min and 55min past.

TRAM (tramalacant.es) narrow gauge railway Alicante–Dénia; daily
Trains leave Alicante daily at 07.19 and hourly at 19 minutes past the hour until 21.19. It takes about 1h30min to Benidorm, where you change for Denia via Calp. Time from Benidorm to Calp is about 35min. Time from Calp to Dénia about 1h. There are plenty of other trains (or bus replacements) at intermediate times which do not cover the full route but might well prove useful for walkers. Downloadable timetables available.

Alicante–Benidorm (to Avinguda Europa) (alsa.es/en) daily
Regular service, about every half hour in both directions from Monday to Friday, about every hour at weekends and holidays.

Benidorm (from Avinguda Europa)–Calp–Dénia (alsa.es/en); daily. Journey time 30mins to Calp; some buses continue to Dénia (+ 1 hour)
Quite frequent; the first buses depart Benidorm:

Mon-Fri	0740	0830	0915
Sat	0815	1020	
Sun	0815	0955	

Benidorm–Finestrat (alicante.avanzagrupo.com/en); Bus No 14 from Rincón de Loix. Journey time 35min. *Recheck times: website down at press date!*
Departs Benidorm 09.15, 15.00; departs Finestrat 07.00,17.00.

Calp–Cala Calalga (autobusesifach.es); daily Bus L1 and L2 (note that bus L3 also goes to Calalga, but continues to Moraira)
Depart Calp TRAM station 07.40 and every half hour until 20.40; the bus stops at Plaza Mayor 10min later (07.50, etc) and in the Plaza Colón two minutes after that (07.52, etc)
Depart Cala Calalga (Maviro/Mercadona/Consum) 08.07 and every half hour until 21.07

Alicante–Alcoi (movilidad.vectalia.es) daily via Castalla, Onil and Ibi (northbound: journey time to Castalla 45min, to Onil 1h, to Ibi 1h15min, to Alcoi 1h45min)
Departs Alicante
Mon-Fri	06.15	08.15	10.00	13.00	15.00	16.45	20.15	21.00
Sat	07.30	10.00	13.15	15.00	18.00	21.00		
Sun	07.00	13.15	19.00					

Departs Alcoi
Mon-Fri	06.15	06.45	08.30	11.00	13.00	14.30	17.00	19.15	21.15
Sat	07.30	10.00	13.15	15.00	18.00	21.00			
Sun	0900	15.00	17.15	21.00					

Puig Campana, with Finestrat to the left (Walk 4)

Ontinyent–Bocairent (laconcepcion.net) 🚐 Line 482

Departs Ontinyent

Mon-Fri	09.20, 16.15, 18.05 (journey time 20min)
Sat	16.17 (journey time 25min)
Sun/holidays	no service

Departs Bocairent

Mon-Fri	06.55, 10.25, 17.18 (journey time 35min)
Sat	08.45 (journey time 35min)
Sun/holidays	no service

Muro de Alcoi–Cocentaina–Alcoi (movilidad.vectalia.es) daily 🚐 (journey time to Cocentaina 15min; journey time to Alcoi 30min)

Departs Muro

Mon-Fri	07.00 to 11.30 every hour, at 30 minutes past the hour
Sat/Sun/hols	09.00, 10.30, 11.30, 15.00, 17.00, 19.00, 21.30

Alicante–Elda (movilidad.vectalia.es) daily 🚐
Alicante–Elda–Petrer–Sax– Villena (journey time to Elda 30min; to Petrer 35min; to Sax 1h; to Villena 1h25min)

Departs Alicante

Mon-Fri	07.50	10.15	12.15	14.30	16.15	19.15 21.20
Sat	10.15	14.15	18.15	20.15		
Sun/hols	11.00	13.15	16.15	18.15	20.15	

Departs Elda

Mon-Fri	07.20	09.00	12.50	15.05	16.50 20.15
Sat	08.45	16.15			
Sun/hols	09.15	16.15			

Alicante–Elda (renfe.es) daily 🚂 (journey time 25-30min). *Note that departure times vary greatly depending on the day of the week; below are just some sample times to show frequency.* Log on to the Renfe website for exact departure and journey times.

Departs Alicante	08.00	10.03	11.08	15.16	18.34
Departs Elda	15.22	17.30	19.30	20.33	21.20

134

Index

Abdet 28
Agres 14, 32, *100-1*, 105, **108**
Aigües de Busot 35
Albir 18, 56, *57*, 133
Alcalà de la Jovada 24, 25
Alcalalí 29
Alcassar 19
Alcoi 14, 30, 31, 43, 99, *100-1*, 104, 133, 134
Alfafara 32
Alicante 36, 133, 134
  town plan 9
Alpatró 26
Altea la Vella 18, 27
L'Atzubia 24, 26, 68, *70-1*, 72
Barranc de Binarreal 80, *81*, 82, **84**
Barranc del Infern *70-1*, 76
Barranc del Sinc 14, 31, 99, *100-1*, 102, **103**
Barranc de la Encantada 25, 65, **66**, *67*
Barranc de las Zorras 112, *114*, 115
El Barxell 33
Bassetes, Ses 50
Benasau 28
Beniardá 14, 28, *87*
Beniarrés 24, 25, **66**
Benidorm 18, 30, 35, 43, 56, *57*, 133, 134
  Playa Levante *8*, 12, 18, 56, *57*
  town plan 8
Benimantell 28, *86*
Benimaurell *70-1*, 74
Benitatxell 19
Bocairent 30, 32, **33**, 96, *97*, 134
Bolulla 23, 77, *78*
Busot 35
Cala Calalga 12, 19, 47, *49*, 50, 133
Cala Fustera 50
Cala Pinet 50
Cala Sardinera 12, 50
Callosa d'En Sarrià 23, 27, *93*, 133
Calp 12, 18, **19**, 27, 47, *49*, 50-1, 52, *53*, 133
Camí de l'Escaleta **96**, *97*, 98
Campbell 22
Cap de la Nau 18, 20, *49*
Cap de Sant Antoni 18, 20, 47, *48*
Cap Prim **11**, 20, 47, *49*
Caprala **2**, 122, 123, *TM*

Casa de Angel 126, 128, *TM*
Casa Foiaderetes 112, *114*
Casa Tancat 13, 78, *79*
Casas de Bixauca 77, *78*
Castalla 15, 36, 37, 126, **128**, 131, 134, *TM*
Castell de Castells 27, 29
Cocentaina 14, 30, 31, 99, *100-1*, 134
Coll de Rates 22
Coll Sabata 99, *100-1*, 102
Confrides 27, 28, 93, *92-3*
Cova de Bolumini *100-1*, 109, 111
Cova de l'Aigua 45, *46*
Cova del Camell 45, *46*
Cova del Rull 24
Cova Tallada 48
Covetes de los Moros 32, 96, *97*, **98**
Coyao, El *116*, 117, 118
Cova de les Calaveres 18, 21
Coves de Canalobre 30, 35
Dénia 18, 20, 24, *46*, 133
  town plan 9
Ebo River 13, 75, 76
Elda 36, 122, 126, 134, *TM*
Ermita de Catí 15, 38, 126, 129, *TM*
Ermita de la Mare de Deu (Agres) 14, 32, 105, 108, *100-1*
Ermita de Santo Cristo (Planes) 65, *67*
Ermita de San Tomás (Serra de Mariola) *100-1*, 109
Ermita Vella 12, 51, *52*
Facheca 28
Famorca **16-7**, 29
Fermosas (plateau) 126, 128, *TM*
Finca Bixauca 13, 77, *78*
Fleix **12**, 13, 18, 22, *70-1*, 73, 74
Font de Partagat 14, 28, *86*, **87**, *92-3*
Font dels Olbits *60-1*, 62, **64**
Font Grota 26, *60-1*, 62
Font Mariola 14, 33, *100-1*, 109
Font Molí 13, 85, *86*
Font Roja (and Parc Natural) 14, 30, 31, 112, **113**, *114*
Font Xili 13, *70-1*
Fonts de L'Algar 13, 18, **23**, 80, *81*
Gallinera (castle) 26, 68, **69**, *70-1*
  Vall de Gallinera 24, 26, *70-1*
Gines *93*
Gorga 27, 28
Guadalest 13, 27, 28, 85, *86*, 92, 134

Presa de Guadalest 28, **90**, *92*
Guadalest River 23, *86*, 91, *92, 93*
Ibi 34, 112, *114*
Isbert, Embalse de *70-1, 73*
Lorcha *see under* L'Orxa
Margarida 25
Mariola (castle) 33, *100-1*, 109; *see also*
    Font
Mas de Fontanerets **108**, 111
Mas de la Cova 15, 34, 119, 120, *121*
Mendivel, El 56, *57*
Molinos, Los 47, *48*
Montforte del Cid 36
Moraira 19, 133
Mountains, rock formations, etc
    Aitana, Serra de **6**, 85, *86*
    Aixorta, Serra de **90**
    L'Arenal 122, **123**, *TM*
    Benicadell, Serra de **4**, **64**, 66
    Bernia, Serra de 29, **53**, 80, *81*
    Campana, Puig 54, *55*, **134**
    Carrasca, Serra de la 43, *70-1, 73-6*
Mountains, etc, *continued*
    Cavall Verd, Serra del **1**, 22
    Despeñador 126, 130, *TM*
    Frare, Serra del (near Biar) 131-2,
    TM
    Frare, Serra del (between Castalla
    and Elda) 126, **128**, *TM*
    Gelada, Serra 12, 18, **56**, *57*, 58
    Maigmó, Serra de 34,   *TM*
    Miserat 68, 69, *70-1*
    Montcabrer 99, *100-1*, 99, 104
    Montgó **11**, 20, **42**, 45, *46; Parc
    Natural del 20-1, **42**, 45, *46*,
    Oltá **19**, *50*
    Penya Mulero *86*
    Penya Sella **88**, *89*
    Penyal d'Ifach 18, **19**, 29
    Portín, El *100-1*, **108**, 109, 110
    Safor,La *60-1*, 62, 63
    Somo, El 77, *78*
Muro de Alcoi 99, *100-1*, 104, 134
Novelda 36
Nucia, La 18, 23
Oltá 12, **19**, *50*
Ontinyent 134
Orba 18, 22
L'Orxa (Lorcha) **4**, 13, 24, 25, 59, *60-
    1*, 62, **63**
Pantanet Gorge 38, 126, 129, *TM*
Parcent 22, 29
Pas dels Bandolers *79*, 82

Pego 24, 26, *70-1*
Pedreguer 18, 21
Penàguila 14, 30, 31, *116*, 117, **118**
Perputxent, Castell de 25, **26**, 59, *60-
    1*, **63**
Petrer 38, 122, *TM*
Planes de la Baronía 13, 24, 25, 66, *67*
Polop 18, 23
Pont de les Calderes (bridge) 25, 65,
    67
Port de la Carrasqueta 14, 34, 119,
    121, 133
Portitxol
    Creu del 12, 20, 47, *9*
    Playa 47, *9*
Pou Clar (spring) *96*, 97
Quatretondeta 27, 28
Racó Llobet 99, *100-1*, 104
Rambla dels Molins 15, 38, 122, 124,
    129, *TM*
Rincón de Loix 18
Sant Cristófol 14, 31, *100-1*
Santuario de la Font Roja 31
Santuario de la Virgin de los Lirios
    114, 115
Santuario de Nuestra Señora de los
    Angeles 12, 20, *48-9*
Sarga, La 15, 34, 119, 120, *121*
Sax 37, 131
Sella 30, *89*
Serpis River 12, 13, 25, **59**, *60-1*
Serras *see* Mountains
Snow wells (see also pages 6-7)
    Cava Arquejada *100-1*, 105, **106**,
    108
    Cava Canyo 112, *114*, 116
    Cava de l'Habitació *100-1*, 105, 106
    Cava Gran *100-1*, **107**, 109
    Cava Simarro *114*, 116
    Caveta del Buitre 7, *100-1*, 108
    Pou de la Noguera 115
    Pou del Surdo 34, **121**, *121*
Tàrbena 13, 22, 29, *80-1*, **cover**
Vall d'Ebo 13, 24, 41, *70-1*, 74, 75
Vall de Laguar 13, 43
Verger 26
La Vila Joiosa 35, 133
Viñalopó River 37, 122,   *TM*
Xàbia 12, 18, 20, 47, *46, 48*, **50**, 133
Xaló/Jalón 27, 29
Xara, La 21
Xixona 34, 133
Xorret de Catí 15, 126, 127, 130, *TM*